Inclusion: STILL the Competitive Business Advantage

by
Shirley Engelmeier

Published by
InclusionINC Media
www.inclusionincmedia.com
Published by eBookIt.com
http://www.eBookIt.com

ISBN-13: 978-1-4566-3222-9

Contents

Dedication

I think about how passionate I am about this work and where that comes from. My tenacity and stick-to-itiveness come from my feisty mom, Mary, who passed early in my process of writing this book. She was a woman born before her time.

My passion is tempered by the good nature of my dad who always seems to put things in perspective with a twinkle in his eye and a contagious laugh. At 93, he is as sharp as any of us reading this book.

Thanks Mom and Dad!

Acknowledgments

A very talented cast assisted with this book, including a number of brilliant business people who contributed their wisdom regarding the necessity of inclusion as a competitive business advantage. To do justice to their accomplishments would have added twenty pages to the book. Instead, I have used their words to breathe life into the concept of inclusion. I thank each of you with a debt of gratitude too large to put into words. Rather than listing you each here, I invite the readers to see on the back of this book a small nugget of your thought leadership. I have used your work extensively throughout this book to make it relevant for business leaders everywhere.

We have the privilege of working with extremely bright business leaders as clients. Thanks to all of you for your validation that inclusion truly is a business strategy.

Closer to home, a heartfelt thank you to Taylor Vernstrom, my millennial whisperer and VP of client solutions. You are by my side day in and day out as my thought partner. To Lin Grensing-Pophal, my editor, thank you for your continued brilliance in shaping this book. Thank you to my brilliant colleagues who implement our work across the globe.

And finally, thank you to the men in my life. Dad, you have grounded not only me, but our family for years. Thanks for that.

To my older son, John Michael, you are still the most stunning young person I know. You are a talented business person well beyond your years.

To my younger son, Zach, a brilliant STEM mind. Your strength of voice, depth of thinking and profound awareness feed my soul.

To my love, Steve, thank you for supporting me and allowing me to live my dream every day.

These and others, too many to name, provide me with ongoing support and inspiration in the work that I do.

INTRODUCTION

Why This Book? Why Now?

Up until this point, you may not have cared about inclusion or diversity. You might have thought it wasn't necessary or mandatory. Then came April 2018 and the announcement of an unemployment rate of 3.9 percent, followed two weeks later by a 3.8 percent unemployment rate and, as of this writing, the rate has fallen even further to 3.7 percent, the lowest in nearly 50 years.[1] Then came the stunning realization that, yes, inclusion does matter; yes, inclusion is a business imperative; yes, inclusion is a must have for engagement, retention, and innovation. Now, it's time to lose sleep. Now it's time to wonder *how are you going to keep your best talent? Who is going to lead your organization for the next five years—the next 10 years?*
How are you going to beat the competition?

Inclusion is a key differentiator for your culture—a culture where all voices are heard. In my work, I'm fortunate to have the opportunity to work and interact with CEOs in every industry. Their insights and perspectives are often compelling and resonate with and reinforce the work we do. As one CEO of an organization of more than 24,000 told me, what keeps him up at night these days is concern about creating a culture where all voices are heard and where his company can compete most effectively. "I want to move faster, so I can say we're doing more," he said. The imperative for companies of all types and sizes today is "to stop the bleeding and retain your stars," particularly in a very competitive employment environment.

And yet, we're not making progress! Despite years of hard work and many good intentions, today's workforce is still fraught with many of the same issues, problems, and concerns we've been talking about and, in theory, taking steps to address. What we're increasingly seeing as we work with companies around the globe is what we're calling the "stuck state"—the point at which many of those who have been involved in this journey for a long time, doing a lot of things, are feeling they're banging their heads against a wall. They're working hard, so why isn't it working?

In 2018, we're still seeing headshots of senior leadership and board members at far too many companies who are all white and

---

[1] https://n.pr/2ykqKSS

all male. This may work if white males represent your market. But, if they don't, you're missing the mark. The makeup of these groups should mirror those you are trying to sell goods and services to now—and in the future.

In 2018, the country is still reeling from an election that has stirred more dissension and vitriolic diatribe toward who the other side is than any other election in recent memory. While we don't get involved in the political landscape, it's impossible to ignore the workplace impacts that growing polarization is creating. We must seek to understand "the other"—especially when "the other" represents the markets we are attempting to serve. We must be inclusive of *all* employees. At a time when we are experiencing a significant cultural divide and innovation is required like never before, harnessing differences is the greatest business need.

In 2018, we're still sending women and people of color to training sessions believing that, somehow, they will get the secret sauce needed to better navigate a culture where they're not the dominant force and not involved in critical decisions about the business or themselves. Generic training sessions addressing the masses don't serve to empower employees to share their views to drive innovation. It's not about sending people to training sessions but about engaging them in managing their own careers. Leaders can be critical catalysts for driving culture change and working to remove, rather than perpetuate, barriers that keep valuable voices silent.

In 2017 and 2018, business headlines repeatedly called out various high-profile companies—Pinterest, Google, Urban Outfitters—for their continued lack of diversity among board members, leaders, and the overall employee community. In fact, Silicon Valley, in general, is a highly visible example of the lack of diversity among tech companies.

Some of these companies' leaders are stepping up to the plate and acknowledging their shortfalls, vying to do something about it. Early in 2018, The Wall Street Journal reported on a memo that Nike's HR chief, Monique Matheson, wrote to staff, saying: "While we've spoken about this many times, and tried different ways to achieve change, we have failed to gain traction—and our hiring and promotion decisions are not changing senior-level representation as quickly as we have wanted."[2]

As we continue to be impacted by the steady, but no longer silent, transformation underway in the demographics of the U.S. and ultimately the American workforce, we simply must stop doing what we've always done to try to address the growing disparities, and increasingly obvious inequities, rampant in our workforce.

The steady increase in diverse workers replacing a historically white population—a shift unlikely just 30 years ago—now marks a new and potentially defining moment in the nation's cultural, geographic, and business DNA: by the middle of this century, the U.S. Census Bureau estimates that minorities will make up nearly 50 percent of the population.

More importantly, the resulting change in population is inexorably linked to the current and future competitiveness of American enterprise. Now more than ever, inclusion must form an integral part of corporate business strategy and culture. The workplace that embraces and leverages variations in perceptions, ideas, and knowledge experiences a level of engagement that can energize productivity, retain highly talented workers, and significantly improve business outcomes.

Though increasing differences in workforce populations make inclusion a significantly more urgent concept than ever before, its highly measurable value is, for the most part, severely under-appreciated. Inclusion remains separate from the strategic part of doing business today. Yet when integrated into the DNA and overall culture of an organization, inclusion can provide a catalyst to gain access to new markets and to attract and keep talent with fresh ideas. Inclusion fuels innovation by ensuring that all voices have not only an opportunity for input, but also the assurance that their voices will be heard—their ideas taken seriously. It's that ability to capture inputs that can help companies be on the cutting edge competitively, that best illustrates the real bottom-line impacts of creating a culture of inclusion. Real benefits are reaped when organizations harness, engage, and connect disparate ideas and experiences to drive productivity, innovation, and competitiveness.

---

[2] https://on.wsj.com/2y3YyEL

Inclusion begins with the creation of a safe, collaborative workplace ecosystem that supports mutual understanding, expression, and regard for different perspectives. Leaders must demonstrate a corporate and holistic commitment to foster this kind of environment, guide the creation of an inclusive culture, and actively align inclusion initiatives with business strategies.

The concept of inclusion extends beyond creating a workplace that focuses solely on representation metrics. It requires the development of formal and informal mechanisms that invite participation and foster genuine contribution to an enterprise's success. Inclusion ensures that employees feel they belong in their places of employment. An inclusive culture for employees means that diverse opinions and ways of doing things are not only acceptable but also embraced as a driver for business! All the efforts you take to build an inclusive culture mean nothing if the end result is that members of various groups—including white males, by the way—don't feel they belong and don't feel their ideas are being heard.

We were pioneers in inclusion work. I founded InclusionINC in 2001. Our name reflects our focus on inclusion—not diversity—as the critical driver for business success. It's not that diversity isn't important; it is. And let's be clear—we are not there yet with diversity! But, it's not enough. Simply gathering together, a group of diverse employees or adding more women and people of color to your C-suite or boardroom isn't enough. It's just a starting point. Building in diversity will achieve nothing if the culture isn't inclusive—if the diverse voices you've brought to the table aren't listened to and their inputs aren't valued.

Inclusion works. Companies with highly integrated and engaged employees demonstrate significantly stronger bottom-line results. In the extremely competitive business environment we are now in—a global environment—the ability to continually innovate is critical, and that can't happen without inclusion! This is more important now than ever, but it also involves innovation with focus and alignment. An organization's inclusion initiatives must be purposely tied to the objectives and mission of the business.

Given our rapidly changing and increasingly uncertain external and internal business environments, there has never been a greater need to hear what all your employees think—not merely your senior leadership team. Not merely your male employees. Not merely your white employees. Not merely "those who know how things get done here." Not merely the employees who agree with you. There has never been a greater need for all voices and ideas to be heard. There has never been a greater need for inclusion.

This is the same stuck state that countless other companies are suffering from. The work has been going on for years, yet the results aren't apparent. If you look at most corporate board members, you'll see a sea of white, male faces—despite the fact that the markets these companies serve are increasingly diverse. This isn't about being nice to women, people of color, or Millennials. It's about how you sell goods and services. How can you effectively meet the needs of your market if you don't understand them? Understanding can only come from listening to people who are *like your market.* We call this *Key Employee Demographics Required for Growth*, and it's about harnessing the best talent available to drive business success.

Business leaders must find a way to capture the insights and visions of people who reflect the growing diversity of consumers, suppliers, and business partners that span the globe. Managers must consider what they may be doing—or not doing —to attract employees and customers in a global context, even if their business is solely focused on U.S. markets. They must learn to harness the collective ideas of the organization to drive business success and create a business ecosystem worth joining.

Against the backdrop of these conditions and the tsunami-like changes occurring demographically in the United States, this book suggests that organizations can realize huge benefits deploying Inclusion is a Business Strategy®, thereby creating a business culture that includes the perspectives of people who don't think like us and often don't look like us, talk like us, or have the same perspectives as us.

Inclusion is about forming a business strategy and culture that:

- Creates a culture where all voices are heard, and all feel a sense of belonging
- Harnesses great ideas to drive innovation
- Expands business thinking to a global mindset for workforce, workplace, and customers

- Considers every single person in the organization as a knowledge worker
- Asks, "Shouldn't inclusion be for everyone?"
- Embraces the technology and collaborative savvy brought to our organizations by members of Gen Y (also known as Millennials, those born between 1980–2000), and Gen Z (those born between 2001 and today)
- Looks forward constantly and never succumbs to complacency

For the sake of clarity, here are the definitions I use for inclusion and diversity. This may be helpful for you in reading this book.

Diversity—noun—describes the differences between people.

Diversity is essentially all the ways in which we differ from one another. Primary dimensions of diversity include age, gender, race, ethnicity, sexual orientation, and physical abilities and qualities. These dimensions of diversity are generally obvious and essentially unchangeable, and they can have a powerful effect on an individual's opportunities.

Diversity also includes dimensions such as socioeconomics, thinking style, personality, educational level, values, religious beliefs, work style, and occupation.

Now, let's contrast that with inclusion.

Inclusion— to include – verb: a call to action—includes everyone's voice and talents.

Inclusion means being open to a variety of ideas, knowledge, perspectives, approaches, and styles from everyone, ensuring that everyone is allowed to bring their best to the workplace to maximize business success.

Now, back to the book…

"Inclusion: STILL the Competitive Business Advantage" sounds the call for a sea change in the approach that organizations take to building and leveraging the diversity of their organizations through inclusion to achieve critical business objectives. Inclusion is a business imperative!

In this updated edition, we'll cover three main areas: why inclusion is still important (chapters 1–5), why inclusion is about business (chapters 6–9) and how inclusion can be an accelerator when it's backed by strategy, powered through accountability, and strengthened through inclusive leadership (chapters 10–12).

I hope this book helps you embrace the significant difference inclusion can make in the success of your business in the twenty-first century.

WHY THIS IS STILL IMPORTANT

1 Why Inclusion Matters More Than Ever

What a difference just a few years make. In April 2018, the unemployment rate dipped to 3.9 percent[3], the lowest since 2000. And then in May 2018, it dropped to 3.8 percent! As the chart below illustrates, the rate has been on a steady decline since a high of 10 percent in 2009—a dramatic illustration of how rapidly the employment climate can change and why organizations must have a *constant* focus on creating a workplace that can attract and retain the best and the brightest. It doesn't pay to take your eye off the ball, as many shortsighted organizations have done during this timeframe.

U.S. Unemployment Rate Dips To 3.9 Percent

Civilian unemployment rate, seasonally adjusted (December 2007 to April 2018)

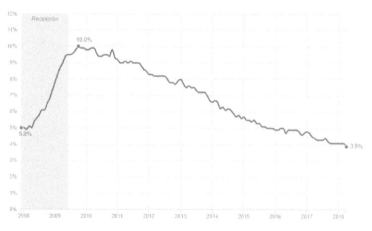

Source: Bureau of Labor Statistics via St. Louis Fed
Credit: NPR

We need only look to the impacts of the #MeToo movement and media coverage of some major inclusion and diversity (I&D) failures at major corporations (e.g., Starbucks, Nordstrom) to recognize how real and relevant inclusion is today—and the impact the failure to create and maintain an inclusive environment can have on organizations. Clearly, even the mighty can fall.

---

[3] https://n.pr/2HOO0jM

In early 2018, a number of shocking situations emerged as the number of incidents of harassment claims continue to rise. An April 2018 headline in The New York Times proclaimed, "At Nike, Revolt Led by Women Leads to Exodus of Male Executives[4]," reporting on a covert survey that was undertaken by a group of women at Nike's headquarters in Beaverton, Oregon, and presented to Nike CEO Mark Parker. Over the following weeks, The New York Times reported, at least six senior executives left the organization, including Trevor Edwards, Nike's president, who had been in line to replace Parker.

The growing number of examples illustrates the importance of inclusion, rather than diversity alone, on the ability to attract, retain, and motivate a workforce that will reflect the faces, perspectives and values of a company's customers. Once again, after the complacency that evolved after 2008's recession, corporate America understands the need to focus on inclusion and diversity!

As Michael Coyle, Pacific Gas & Electric's principal program manager for diversity and inclusion, told me as I was working on this book, working in the field of inclusion and diversity at this time represents "the best of times and the worst of times with unprecedented change and demand."

I can understand his point of view. For over 25 years, I've worked with organizations to address inclusion as a business strategy. Prior to this, I spent more than 15 years in large organizations and held executive-level positions at Brown & Williamson and Frito-Lay. I cut my teeth on corporate assignments at these organizations developing programs for national rollout, which impacted all levels of field activities. I was responsible for implementing these programs to all levels, and I'm as comfortable speaking with frontline staff as I am with CEOs and COOs. Ultimately, I opted out of Corporate America and eventually began my own consulting firm to avoid the hardships required of women in pursuit of career advancement at that time. My work with Fortune 500 companies has encompassed a broad range of industries and organizations, including Intuitive Surgical, BASF, ESPN, Denny's/Advantica, 3M, Cargill, Michelin, Campbell Soup and Mortenson

---

[4] https://nyti.ms/2JDQH3R

Construction to name a few. It's work I'm passionate about. Unfortunately, it's also work that proceeds in fits and starts, with progress often seeming elusive. Although we have been able to partner with our clients to help them achieve significant progress, here we are, decades after we first started this work, still seeing many companies showing little progress collectively for the broad-based effort that has been called diversity.

When I wrote the first edition of this book in 2012, we were still reeling from the effects of the recession, which took hold in 2008. For several years, we saw diversity initiatives thrown under the bus in cost-cutting measures because the business linkage had not been made. This was highly unfortunate because that business linkage has become increasingly valuable—and increasingly real!

The good news is that some of this is beginning to change.

Two tactics that have been employed under the diversity umbrella are a targeted focus on recruitment strategies and a singular emphasis on training. While hiring women and people of color is a historic tactic for achieving a diverse workforce, it is only part of the equation. In order to drive change, those individuals with differences need to come to a culture that welcomes their input and is inclusive. Targeted hiring remains critical, but no sustainable change will occur until senior leaders leverage the business connection between diversity and the bottom line.

For years, much of Corporate America has been focused only on the concept of diversity—i.e., race and gender—and hasn't gotten the bigger picture of changing the workplace culture to one of inclusion – an inclusion that leverages the benefits of diversity for business gains. More significantly, inclusion and diversity haven't been treated as mission critical; they haven't been linked to business outcomes.

Add to this the *highly disruptive times we live in.* We now live and work in an environment where disruption is the new business normal!

- We are faced with great uncertainty from a variety of forces—economic, natural, and political.
- We are faced with the convergence of technology and new thought processes being brought to the workforce by the

younger, highly influential members of Gen Y and, most recently, Gen Z, who want to participate, not just execute.
- We are faced with the need to continually innovate and use all our assets to keep up with domestic and global competition.
- We are faced with radical demographic changes; both in the U.S. and globally, that affect our competitiveness and our markets. In fact, for many U.S. organizations, their greatest growth is coming from outside the U.S.
- We are faced with a shrinking labor pool and the lowest unemployment rates we have seen in years.
- We are faced with geopolitical influences and the changing dominance of economic powerhouses.

The list goes on and on.

Living in this rapidly changing, disruptive global environment begs for inclusion and inclusive leadership. And yet the vast majority of U.S. companies are not taking advantage of the power of inclusion because of a confluence of four conditions:

1. Lack of a strategic linkage between workplace demographics and business outcomes.
2. Technology that, unlike in any other era, has made it possible for customers, suppliers, and employees to communicate in ways never expected.
3. Diverse employees who, despite the gains made by diversity initiatives of the past, remain in lower tiers of business where their influence is much less than that of senior managers.
4. A state of stuck in which leaders who have been spinning their wheels for years without progress simply don't know what to do next. In that state of stuck, many stop.

Oh, and by the way, this is really hard work! We need to lift up the blind spots or biases that are systemic and perpetuated by organizational leadership unintentionally. *Yes*, unintentionally. No one wakes up in the morning and thinks, "I'm going to overlook critical talent that is different from me!" That's where leadership must become open to the unconscious biases they have and openly begin to have conversations about how these biases impact talent and pipeline development.

And yet, bias, however unintentional, continues to be pervasive in Corporate America. There are plenty of statistics to illustrate the lack of diversity across all industries and at all levels of leadership, up to and including board representation. The point is more poignantly driven home, though, by these observations in a piece from The Upshot[5], which provides a list of the top jobs where Fortune 500 CEO women are outnumbered by men named John!

And it appears that we're losing more ground: The percentage of female Fortune 500 CEOs dropped by 25 percent in 2018, according to Fortune[6].

Hiring women and people of color has never been important simply for the sake of political correctness or because it is the right thing to do. The goal has always been a two-sided coin—attracting and retaining the best talent for the benefit of the business as well as opening the doors of opportunity across the entire demographic spectrum. Much has changed since I wrote the first edition of this book in 2012—most notably the talent landscape. From the days of the employer's market in 2008 to around 2010, when unemployment began to decline, executives currently find themselves wondering who will lead their organizations now and in the future.

The war for talent has never been so intense. The big takeaway in a tight employment environment is this—make sure to capitalize on the diversity that you are (or should be) building within your organization. Don't ignore the potential of women and people of color; if you do, you do so at your own peril!

An inclusive culture is critical to ensure that diverse candidates can not only be hired, but also be retained and developed. One tactic that has been broadly used is training. The one-time training event that occurs every three to seven years (a "dip-and-done" approach) has seen better days. Corporate America has needed, and still needs, an accelerated learning strategy associated with new inclusion business behaviors and a new underlying paradigm of what inclusion and, yes, diversity mean to business success.

---

[5] https://nyti.ms/2qVat41

[6] https://for.tn/2KHxgbf

Another specific area of need continues to be developing inclusive leadership competencies among those who are responsible for leading others—this must be done from the top of the organization on down. There should be no assumptions made that senior leaders, or those with many years of business experience, have inclusive leadership competencies. All too often they do not. Again, training efforts cannot be a dip-and-done undertaking. The training must be ongoing, occurring over time. Those in leadership positions should also be held accountable, evaluated, and continually coached to ensure these skills take root in the organization. They must develop inclusive leadership competencies that will ensure they have the mindset, values, and skills to include all members of their teams.

I know without a doubt that inclusion is a key to business success. I began working in this arena over 25 years ago, as a white woman on Denny's racial discrimination consent decree. My esteemed colleagues and I worked for two and a half years to correct the ills of a major class action lawsuit. I'm especially proud of this as a white woman from Minnesota. The punch line here is we were able to help Denny's think through why more effective behavior mattered for their business! In the mid '90s, we were already talking about inclusion and diversity as keys to business success. When I founded InclusionINC in 2001, the brand promise was highly focused on the critical importance of inclusion as key to business success because it was clear, even then, that diversity by itself was only part of the story.

While diversity is certainly linked to inclusion, organizations can be diverse and not inclusive. This body of work began with a primary focus on race, gender, and representation metrics; that's the diversity side of it. Inclusion is the other side of the diversity coin, and, yet, inclusion is so much bigger than that.

Today, the reality is that diversity goes beyond race and gender to include the coexistence in the workplace of five generational cohorts at a time when everyone's voice is needed to drive employee engagement, innovation, and market agility. The global mindset for business and cross-cultural communication requires an understanding of diversity and differences.

The need for creating a culture of inclusion is critical against this backdrop of diverse employees and diverse customers. Focusing on inclusion as a business strategy helps drive innovation, engagement, and productivity and keeps the best talent. Inclusion helps to sell more goods and services. Inclusion is a business imperative!

2 The Impact of Radical, Seismic Demographic Shifts

For Sodexo, inclusion is a choice, says Sandy Harris, former Vice President of Global Diversity and Inclusion. "It's an intentional focus on acting for the growth and well-being of our people." Sodexo's business model is different from many other companies—their staff members reside in client sites across a wide range of industries—from healthcare, to education, to sports and leisure, corporate services, the government, and more. Diversity comes with the territory.

But the workplace is changing for every organization; change is being driven by radical and seismic demographic shifts that impact both the available labor market and the consumer market. Businesses can't afford to ignore the potential impacts of these shifts on their ability to attract and retain top talent—and to attract customers.

Baby boomers, poised on the precipice of retirement long beyond their predicted presence in the workforce, are moving on while Millennials represent the dominant players in the workplace and Generation Z follows fast on their heels. And, Gen X, in many regards the "lost generation," is finally poised to step up and take on the leadership roles they have so long clamored for.

The ethnic and cultural diversity of the country also continues to grow and shift.

All these changes impact how businesses recruit, lead and market their goods and services. Inclusion *is* a business imperative.

A Younger Workforce Demographic

Millennials (also known as Gen Y) represent the biggest bubble in population demographics since the Baby Boomers. Their impact on the workforce has been significant. They became the largest generation in the labor force in 2016 and maintain their dominance today. "More than one-in-three American labor force participants (35 percent) are Millennials, making them the largest generation in the U.S. labor force, according to a Pew Research Center analysis of U.S. Census Bureau data."[7]

Generation Z is nipping at their heels, though, and will become the next generation to watch as they begin to make their mark on the workforce. Pew's analysis also indicates that Generation Z, which they refer to as post-Millennials (born after 1996), currently comprise 5 percent of the labor force.

Millennials became the largest generation in the labor force in 2016

U.S. labor force, in millions

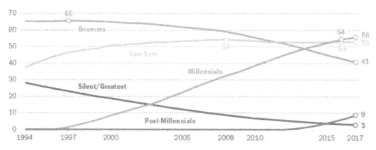

Note: Labor force includes those ages 16 and older who are working or looking for work. Annual averages shown.
Source: Pew Research Center analysis of monthly 1994-2017 Current Population Survey (IPUMS).

PEW RESEARCH CENTER

---

[7] https://pewrsr.ch/2qn2Pz0

More than a third of the workforce are Millennials

% of the U.S. labor force

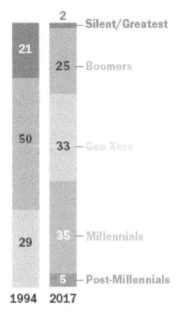

1994   2017

Note: Labor force includes those ages 16 and older who are working or looking for work. Annual averages shown. Source: Pew Research Center analysis of monthly 1994 and 2017 Current Population Survey (IPUMS).

PEW RESEARCH CENTER

Both generations are characterized by some striking differences between them and the cohorts that preceded them. They are more likely to be comfortable with technology, less likely to be loyal to organizations than generations before, demanding more work-life balance, and eager to have their voices heard. They demand a different type of management than their older colleagues and, indeed, as Millennials themselves enter the leadership ranks, according to Jeff Fromm, an expert on Millennials and

Generation Z writing for Forbes, tells us that 83 percent of today's managers are Millennials![8]

They are, in fact, changing the face of management, as Brad Karsh points out in "Manager 3.0[9]: A Millennial's Guide to Rewriting the Rules of Management." As managers, they are, he says, "creative, big thinkers and they will change the face of leadership—*if* they can bridge the gap between the hierarchical management style of senior executives and the casual, more collaborative approach of their peers." They are certainly trying!

As Sodexo's Harris told us: "Diversity is what it is—it is a fact. There is a mix of people coming together to do business. We want to be able to attract end users—customers and consumers. Diversity and inclusion make that possible. When we think about communication and the marketplace, D&I is core to our brand promise. We are well known for our efforts."

Patricia Rossman, Chief Diversity and Inclusion Officer at BASF North America, also emphasizes the radical shifts in the North American talent market as a big driver of the company's focus not only on hiring diverse candidates, but also on being mindful of the importance of inclusion and the value that a multitude of diverse voices and perspectives can bring to the organization. "This is a business-focused strategy for BASF and we are increasingly focused on using inclusion to fully leverage the diversity that we're working so hard to bring in."

The Aging of the U.S. Population

According to a report from the Population Reference Bureau (PRB)[10], the number of Americans aged 65 and older will more than double by 2060—about one-quarter of Americans will be over 65. As Boomers try to leave the workforce in what has become a very tight labor market, some employers are taking steps to actively court them. Take Mercedes, for instance. They are working to keep the Boomer population in Germany because they, like the U.S., face the challenges of an aging society and a

---

[8] https://bit.ly/2CyUGj5

[9] https://amzn.to/2Nw2eUv

[10] https://bit.ly/2C4fj5o

shrinking labor force.[11] Some organizations are working hard to keep the Boomers they have and are reaching out to recruit other members of an aging workforce—a prime example of how inclusion, of *everyone*, is a business imperative!

The mass exodus of Boomers predicted years ago is starting to take hold, and organizations are finding themselves challenged to replace their numbers, despite the significance of the millennial generation. Millennials' quest for work-life balance may be one of the drivers of an increasing focus on work-life balance. According to a Monster.com article:[12] "Many in the 'latchkey generation'[13] are at a life stage with children and some must care for aging parents, too. For these workers, workplace flexibility and work/life balance are critical components of the decision to stay in, or step away from, the workforce."[14]

Employers are already finding themselves struggling to replace retiring staff members—a situation that may continue for years to come. The impact of an aging generation is compounded by the lowest U.S. birth rates in 30 years. The population is not renewing itself, according to a report in The Hill. "The U.S. is now officially an 'aging society,' one in which the proportion of the population over 65 exceeds that under age 15."

Age demographics represent a rather sharp dichotomy between younger and older population segments. According to research from the Employee Benefit Research Institute, reported in HR Dive, "the 55-and-older share of the labor force will keep growing in the short term due to the generation's size."[15]

The Browning of America

Age isn't the only demographic that is seeing a rapid rise in diversity at both ends of the spectrum.

---

11 https://reut.rs/2trjgfq

12 https://bit.ly/2yUvIOE

13 https://bit.ly/2QFd9NR

14 https://bit.ly/2zZpnve

15 https://bit.ly/2IPxVGO

At the same time, the proportion of minorities in the U.S. is increasing significantly. The Selig Center for Economic Growth[16] estimates that "in 2017, 20 million Americans—6.1 percent of the country's population—will claim Asian ancestry, which makes the group a powerful force in the U.S. consumer market. This racial group's shares of the population were 3 percent, 4 percent, 5.2 percent, and 6.1 percent in 1990, 2000, 2010, and 2017, respectively; and their enormous economic clout continues to attract more attention from businesses and advertisers."

"From 2000 to 2017, the nation's black population grew by 21.7 percent compared to 9.4 percent for the white population and 15.8 percent for the total population. From 2017 to 2022, the nation's black population is projected to grow by 5.9 percent, which exceeds the 4.3 percent growth estimated for the total U.S. population."

We have reached the tipping point.

The long-term impact of the changes in growth is further evident when looking at the trend analysis that follows. By 2050, the U.S. Census projects that non-Hispanic whites will make up 52.5% of the population. At this point, nearly half of the U.S. population will be racially or ethnically different than it was just a short time ago.

Clearly, businesses today are dealing with a constantly changing mix of people and perspectives that often present challenges, both for management and for employees themselves. Shifts are happening in gender, age, and ethnicity; these factors impact the makeup of the workplace and the population at large.

These seismic demographic shifts in the U.S. population hold both peril and promise for Corporate America. They hold peril for those who fail to recognize and take steps to embrace the diversity of a changing employee and customer landscape, but they hold promise for those who, through inclusion, can capitalize on the significant potential these populations hold for them.

---

[16] The Multicultural Economy 2017 - Jeffrey M. Humphreys, Selig Center for Economic Growth

Buying Power/U.S. Emerging Markets

Not only will these demographic shifts have important implications for the makeup of the future workforce, but they will also influence the corporate customer base. The Selig Center for Economic Growth indicates that the impact of diverse markets will be significant. Let's take a closer look at the numbers below.

Selig's report[17], "The Multicultural Economy", indicates that "in 2017, the combined buying power of blacks, Asians, and Native Americans will be $2.4 trillion—156 percent higher than its 2000 level of $926 billion—which amounts to a gain of $1.4 trillion.

African Americans will account for 54 percent of this spending, according to the report.

In fact, the increase of all segments is higher than the projected buying power of the white population.

Capturing Growth Markets

Buying Power (Billions of Dollars)

	2000	2010	2017	2022	%increase 2017-2022
White	6,413.5	9,434.5	11,998.1	14,127.2	17.5%
Black	608.9	957.4	1,268.7	1,536.3	21.1%
Hispanic	494	1,015	1,494	1,928	29.0%
American Indian	40.3	82.4	112.8	139.4	23.6%
Asian	276.5	605.7	986.2	1,345.5	36.4%
Multiracial	60.2	141.5	212.2	287.0	35.2%

Source: Selig Center for Economic Growth, Multicultural Economy 2017

To put these impacts into perspective, consider this. In 2017, according to The Selig Center[18], the $1.5 trillion Hispanic market was larger than the entire economies of all but 12 countries in the world.

---

[17] Selig - ibid

[18] Selig - ibid

Still under the illusion that you don't need to be concerned about the minority market segments that are rapidly growing to become the majority? Still think running a few focus groups a year will let you know how to market and sell to a Latino or African American audience?

And think about this - these numbers are likely to grow exponentially over the next decade.

This paints a picture of rapidly changing consumer demand for products and services that meet the expectations of a wide range of market segments that have never before been served in the U.S. At the same time, businesses in the U.S. are no longer just impacted by the U.S. economy. They are increasingly impacted by an equally rapidly growing and interactive global economy as well.

What do I see happening on a global level? Emerging markets and rapidly changing global consumerism are creating an economic imperative that seems evident to most businesses. Yet, while apparent, this opportunity is not so readily addressed. This disconnect occurs because the employee population doesn't necessarily reflect the new and emerging consumer, both in the U.S. and globally. Inclusion is a necessary business strategy to tap these opportunities.

Unfortunately, the dots, to date, have not been connected despite multiple studies showing that diversity matters from a business perspective. For instance, an article by Lisa Wardell in Chief Executive points to the following research.

- "McKinsey & Company found companies with strong gender diversity among their executives were 21 percent more likely to outperform on profitability compared with peers.
- They found the same held true for ethnic and cultural diversity among executives, whose teams were 33 percent more likely to lead in profitability in their industry.
- A study by Gallup of two large corporations in the retail and hospitality sectors found increases of 14 percent in comparative revenue and 19 percent in higher net profit

respectively in gender-diverse business units versus less gender-diverse business units."[19]

Both diversity and inclusion are at the core of business, says Rossman of BASF. "There are all kinds of studies that show the link between the diversity of your workforce and profitability and bottom line performance." BASF knows, she says, that while competitors may be able to replicate, to a certain extent, a company's products and processes, what they can't so effectively replicate "is that special spark, that special chemistry that your people bring to their work to drive your customers' success."

Donald Fan, Walmart's Senior Director in the Global Office of Culture, Diversity and Inclusion, also points to the McKinsey report as strongly supportive of the business case for diversity. The research, he says, "proves why diversity and inclusion, especially building and fostering an inclusive environment, workplace and culture, are so critical to business success in today's environment."

Faced with radical and seismic demographic shifts, what is the imperative for today's businesses? Inclusion. Inclusion is a business strategy that capitalizes on radical and seismic demographic shifts, mining the talent from groups whose diversity encompasses age, gender, culture, socioeconomic backgrounds, and more.

---

[19] https://bit.ly/2pNzBs8

3 The Global Mindset

Just as the buying power of newly emerging and increasingly diverse populations in America is projected to change significantly over the next few decades, the ability of citizens of less developed nations to purchase consumer goods and services is also projected to markedly increase between now and 2050.

John Hawksworth of PricewaterhouseCoopers shows compelling evidence of this shift in "The Long View: How will the global economic order change by 2050?", published in 2017.[20] The following chart shows the dramatic change from 2016–2050 for some of the world's largest developing economies.

	2016	2050	
China	1	1	China
US	2	2	India
India	3	3	US
Japan	4	4	Indonesia
Germany	5	5	Brazil
Russia	6	6	Russia
Brazil	7	7	Mexico
Indonesia	8	8	Japan
UK	9	9	Germany
France	10	10	UK

☐ E7 economies   ◼ G7 economies

---

[20] https://pwc.to/2A0j5LU

It's a landscape that is continually shifting as companies—and countries—vie to maintain a foothold in a radically changing global economy.

Changes in Economic Influence

Any doubt that the global market is having an impact on the success of companies here in the U.S. can be dispelled by looking at data showing where the top company headquarters are located. The number of Fortune Global 500 companies headquartered in the U.S. declined from 179 (36 percent) in 2000 to 132 (26 percent) in 2017 while the number of companies headquartered in China grew from 10 to 109 over this same time period.[21]

There is no question that global trade is of critical importance to the United States and other countries as they seek to be competitive in a world economy. What is hampering the United States' efforts to capitalize on these world markets? I suggest it is the failure to first capitalize on the power of its employees. This must be a mindful process, recognizing that inclusion means listening to a wide range of diverse voices and inputs and recognizing that this input is powerful from a bottom-line business perspective.

Why does this matter? Our current U.S. workforce does not reflect the face of these changing markets. As emerging markets grow, we need to consider whether our existing workforce can address emerging global needs. In many cases today, it cannot.

McKinsey research[22] provides insights into the representation of women and people of color along the employment continuum from entry level to the C-suite. The results are telling. For instance, while white men represent only 36 percent of entry-level workers, that number rises to 68 percent by the time they hit the C-suite. Conversely, white women represent 31 percent of entry-level workers, but only 19 percent of the C-suite. The numbers are even more dismal for people of color as the chart below indicates:

---

[21] https://go.ey.com/2tuxQTi

[22] https://mck.co/2JDFH8c

REPRESENTATION IN THE CORPORATE PIPELINE BY GENDER AND RACE

% OF EMPLOYEES BY LEVEL IN 2018[1]

	ENTRY LEVEL	MANAGER	SR. MANAGER/ DIRECTOR	VP	SVP	C-SUITE
WHITE MEN	36%	46%	52%	59%	67%	68%
MEN OF COLOR	16%	16%	13%	12%	9%	9%
WHITE WOMEN	31%	27%	26%	24%	19%	19%
WOMEN OF COLOR	17%	12%	8%	6%	4%	4%
% WOMEN 2018 PIPELINE	48%	38%	34%	29%	23%	22%
CHANGE '17–'18	1%	1%	1%	0%	2%	2%
CHANGE '16–'17	1%	0%	0%	0%	-3%	1%
CHANGE '15–'16	1%	0%	1%	2%	1%	2%

McKinsey&Company

Yet, despite these findings, McKinsey also indicates that organizations' diversity goals and priorities won't change significantly over the next three years and that, while significant progress has been made to build and retain diverse workforces, there are still significant inroads to be made.

The report concludes, "The globalization of business has created a sophisticated, complex and competitive environment. In order to be successful, companies need to continually create new products and services. And the best way to ensure the development of new ideas is through a diverse and inclusive workforce."

Relying on your current workforce to reach new markets may work in the short term, but as markets evolve, businesses will need to call upon an increasingly technologically savvy and connected global workforce. This is not and cannot be a U.S.-centric model.

To capture emerging markets, businesses need to develop a highly engaged global workforce and mindset that understands:

- Who their current customers are
- Who their emerging customers are

- What their current and emerging customers' needs, values, and preferences are
- Why and how their customers access their services
- How to communicate effectively with their customers
- How to customize products and services based on demand

This is the new business normal. Until organizations can respond effectively to the new normal, nobody wins:

- Not the employees who are unable to lend their expertise and passion in support of their organizations' marketing
- Not the organizations that hire diverse workers but don't involve them
- Not the customers whose experiences with various organizations might have been more valuable if those organizations had listened to the voices of all their constituents

According to a PricewaterhouseCoopers survey of more than 1,293 CEOs in 85 countries (104 in the U.S.), CEOs don't see globalization going away, but they do see it changing. In the report "US Business Leadership in the World in 2018[23]," the countries identified as holding the most opportunity for international growth are China (47 percent), the UK (30 percent), and Germany (27 percent).

The "fracturing of the foundation" of globalization, says the report, "will fundamentally alter the regulatory and risk landscape that business leaders face over the next two to three years."

Respondents' concerns are outlined in the following chart from the report.

---

[23] https://pwc.to/2GX5W7R

Q. Do you believe the world is moving more towards...

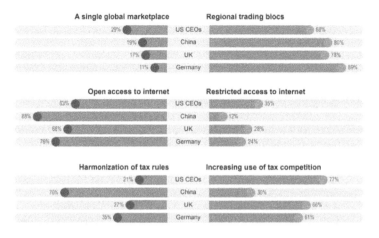

Source: PwC, 21st Annual Global CEO Survey -US supplement
Base: US CEO respondents (104); China (162); UK (193); Germany (48)

What is one of the top areas of focus to support faster growth? Staff. According to this report, "US CEOs are hiring for broadly relevant digital skills and collaborative, creative and efficient work styles. They're investing in continuous learning initiatives (39 percent) to reduce employee churn and provide development paths for employees to add skills."

CEOs are critically, and appropriately, concerned not just with the ability to hire employees—many representing highly skilled, and highly in-demand types of competencies that are in short supply—but also with the ability to *retain* those employees. Retention requires inclusion from the outset of their employment throughout the employee life cycle.

There has been a shift in the strength of global markets since 2012, when my first book was released. At that time, the focus was on BRICS (Britain, Russia, India, China and South Africa). But, as Ian Bremmer pointed out in a 2017 Time article[24], "even the sturdiest of BRICS isn't as strong as it used to be." Why? He points to some key factors:

- The global financial crisis inflicted lasting damage; "Goldman Sachs shut down its BRIC investment fund in

_____

[24] https://ti.me/2iQtuTN

late 2015 after its assets plunged in value by 88 percent from their 2010 highpoint," Bremmer writes.
- The fall in commodity prices created significant damage.
- Corruption continues to be "endemic" within the BRICS.
- Even the "winners" among the BRICS countries, India and China, remain at risk and vulnerable to the impacts of poverty. "The World Bank estimates that 68 percent of all existing Jobs in India are 'at risk' from automation. In China, the figure is 77 percent," says Bremmer.

Once again, world events illustrate the importance of a continued focus on the major economic, cultural and social impacts that affect organizations' ability to remain viable.

As global brands seek to serve new markets, they recognize the need to modify their products to appeal to global tastes. This is in sharp contrast to the approach that Harvard Business School professor Theodore Levitt declared in a 1983 HBR article, "The Globalization of Markets." At that time, Levitt was pushing the idea of "a global market for uniform products and services," arguing that companies should "exploit the 'economics of simplicity' and grow by selling standardized products all over the world."

That, of course, didn't happen. In their 2004 Harvard Business Review article referencing Levitt's thoughts on how global brands compete, authors[25] Douglas Holt, John Quelch, and Earl L. Taylor write: "The forces that Levitt described didn't produce a homogeneous world market; they produced a global culture," and pointed out that "the rise of a global culture doesn't mean that consumers share the same tastes or values."

From our 2019 vantage point, it's shocking to think that the concept of market homogeneity ever took root! In fact, some of the most successful global firms took the exact opposite approach—seeking to appeal to local tastes and preferences in the markets they chose to serve or expand into, not only in their products but also in their communication strategies and messaging.

International companies expanding into the U.S. market have also found that they must localize their offerings to appeal to

---

[25] https://bit.ly/1ADbv0g

U.S. consumers. Toyota is one extremely successful example[26]. "Like other successful models for global marketing, Toyota built a strong, recognizable brand and then customized it to meet local market needs. Using international manufacturing techniques backed by an uncompromising branding model, the company became the world's best-selling car manufacturer."

These same shifts are being seen in the U.S., as global players recognize that even here at home, the population is increasingly fragmented. Interestingly, not only do global segments within the United States have an interest in foods reminiscent of their cultures, U.S. consumers are developing tastes for new ethnic foods that various ethnic groups are popularizing. While Italian, Mexican and Chinese food remain U.S. favorites, according to Nation's Restaurant News[27], Americans are being introduced to, and enjoying, foods like kombucha (a fermented drink made from a Manchurian mushroom), fish sauce (a condiment popular in southeast and eastern Asian countries), Aleppo pepper (a spice from the Middle East), and more.

Localization has also become a key economic trend, creating a global/local dichotomy. While global trends still resonate with consumers, the go-local movement also continues to drive consumer shopping preferences even, interestingly, toward person-to-person, brick-and-mortar interactions, according to PwC's "Global Consumer Insights Survey (GCIS)[28]," conducted in late 2017. As reported by Strategy+Business[29], "GCIS respondents told us for the fourth year in a row that they have increased, not decreased, their shopping in physical stores." Consumers, according to the study, "are complex; conflicted; highly segmented by age, gender, and geography; and on the cusp of change."

Even as they go global, companies increasingly understand that they must go local. There is no mass market anymore. Today's companies, even those in industries where products presumably appeal to the masses (packaged goods, cars, computers and other

---

[26] https://bit.ly/2CdlfIt

[27] https://bit.ly/2yq3sLx

[28] https://pwc.to/2pd9muK

[29] https://bit.ly/2xYYTsg

technology, etc.), must focus not only their products but also their messaging, to engage niche audiences.

At Michelin, for instance, Herb Johnson, Jr., Chief Diversity and Inclusion Officer for Michelin North America, says that the company's Hispanic network has been "very instrumental in partnering with our recruiting teams to attend campus visits at the University of Texas at El Paso, and to support our Hispanic employees in our Oklahoma facility and our two facilities in Mexico."

General Motor's focus on accountability and meaningful metrics like its "ethnic share of brand," which we'll discuss more in chapter 8 is another great example of focusing on key niche markets and working to understand them to drive key business results.

Being attuned to emerging market segments, and shifts in consumer preferences, in the U.S. and globally can help companies increase market share to existing untapped new markets in the U.S. and new markets around the world.

Certainly, it can be challenging to manage an organization across multiple geographies and multiple markets, but the efforts pay off. At Sodexo, Harris works with a very sophisticated and very matrixed network of global players focused on diversity and inclusion coordinated from the top of the global organization by a Global Chief Diversity Officer in partnership with the Group Executive Committee (global senior leadership team), Segment Leaders, global Regional Leadership Chairs, and Global HR. The Regional Leadership Committees drive the work across the various business segments at the country level. EBRGs (Employee Business Resource Groups), Networks and Councils sit at the grassroots level. Communication and coordination across these groups helps Sodexo stay attuned to emerging employee, and market, needs.

Whether working in a multinational organization or a firm with operations and markets only in the U.S., companies today must have a global mindset. The business benefit is twofold: meeting the needs of emerging markets and growing the demand for new products among existing markets. Brilliant! And chances are, the most enlightened brands found the seeds of innovation and customization from insights gleaned internally through employee input—the kind of rich input that only emerges from inclusive organizations. Inclusion drives business performance and growth.

4 The War for Talent

As I work with CEOs around the country, I benefit from their unique in-the-trenches insights on how their businesses are being impacted by seismic shifts such as the war for talent. One CEO told me, as I was working on this book, that the unemployment rate—which is the lowest it's been in 17 years—is what's keeping most CEOs up at night these days. "It's so hard to replace good talent lost," he says. Companies must "stop the bleeding and retain their stars." But how? He says that companies need to "create a culture where all voices are heard to compete most effectively. "Set the right tone and the right culture." Reinvigorating the war for talent, he says, requires "being ahead of the game and planning for the next five to 10 years."

According to The Conference Board's "C-Suite Challenge 2018" report[30], the top concern of CEOs—and other members of the C-suite—is attracting and retaining talent. The second, closely related, is creating new business models to address disruptive technologies. Those disruptive technologies are driving demand for new types of very specialized talent that is generally in short supply. Organizations today can't risk turning off job candidates or new hires—or long-term staff members.

Molly Weiss, Senior Director of HR with Mortenson Construction in Minneapolis, says: "We have been incredibly intentional about making sure we're attracting the very best talent in the marketplace, and we know that the very best talent comes from all different sources. We need to be very thoughtful about tapping into those sources." Mortenson, she says, made a very intentional push in 2016 with its recruiting team to ensure they were doing outreach to groups they hadn't reached out to in the past. That, she says, led to "an increase in our candidate pool and in our hires—eventually we were able to tap into some new sources of talent."

Doing that effectively, though, requires the identification of and elimination of barriers.

---

[30] https://bit.ly/2mRCMOS

BARRIER #1 – Bias in the Recruiting Process

The recruiting process itself is often fraught with bias, however unintentional. As a Fast Company article, "Are You Making One of These Recruiting Mistakes That Show Bias," notes, some very simple mistakes are common. Author Gwen Moran points to the following:

- Requiring unnecessary credentials or job experience. Doing so can disproportionately impact the number of women and people of color who may apply for open positions. Women, in fact, have been shown to be less likely to "raise their hands and submit for candidacy when they feel that they are a 50 percent to 60 percent job fit," the article notes. Being overly stringent and setting a bar that's too high will limit your opportunity to recruit diverse candidates who can bring new perspectives and insights.
- Not having the talk with your recruiters. The point here: don't assume that your recruiters know what your goals are in terms of recruiting diverse candidates. Have the conversation.
- Choosing biased advertising parameters. Where this misstep has most reared its head is in relation to older workers. As the Fast Company article points out: "In December 2017, a joint investigation by ProPublica and the New York Times found that a number of high-profile companies were using Facebook ad-targeting tools to block older workers from seeing job ads."
- Using off-putting language in job postings and interviews. Some examples Moran gives based on input from Lucia Smith, an HR consultant, are terms or phrases like "rock star," "ninja," "work hard/play hard," and "hardcore"—"all signs that your culture is a bit 'bro-y' or not welcoming to people with families or other responsibilities." Another example: "Social media management firm Buffer found that eliminating the word 'hacker' from software developer job descriptions made them more appealing to women." The lesson here: watch your language! Even using such seemingly innocuous terms as "expert" can limit your opportunity to draw from a larger and more diverse pool—as noted earlier, women,

for instance, are less likely to "raise their hand" when the bar seems too high.[31]

What's interesting about this list is that nearly *every one* of these items is also part of the talent management process. Those who make their way to the high-potential lists are those who get promoted and who get tapped for the succession plan. Bias in recruiting impacts employees at every stage in the employment life cycle, minimizing the positive potential that inclusion can have for the organization.

Much of this bias is unintentional, says Rossman with BASF. As the BASF team drilled down to examine the numbers related to the North American talent pool, which has been becoming increasingly diverse, and examined the candidate pool hiring managers were drawing from to interview, "we recognized that while we were seeing an appreciable uptick in diverse applicants, our talent pool was not becoming appreciably more diverse, or not at the same pace that we would expect," she says. There were two things that impacted this, she said: a preference for too many very specific job requirements that screened out some great talent, and unconscious bias among hiring managers.

"We found that we would have job specifications or job requirements that included about 15 -16 very rigid requirements that narrowed the lens too much." In fact, so much, she says, "that only the incumbent could qualify for that job—this wasn't intended to leave out great talent, but it was the result." BASF has, subsequently, narrowed those requirements to a best practice goal of no more than five.

Another impact, says Rossman, reflected "human nature 101— we tend to interview and hire ourselves. Unconscious bias was really showing up in our selection process—not deliberately, but the results were not what we wanted."

BARRIER #2 – The Slippery Slope of Meritocracy

Employers and their HR advisors are quick to proclaim that their hiring and promotion decisions are merit-based. Yet, when some practical logic is applied to these claims, their arguments quickly

---

[31] https://bit.ly/2Fr27X4

fall apart, as Tim Wise, the author of "White Like Me: Reflections on Race from a Privileged Son"[32] frequently points out. When people assert that a country, an industry or an organization is meritocratic, and that people are selected to fill various roles based on merit, it begs a larger question and, perhaps, signals not-so-subtle signs of racism or sexism. Why? Because if a company says its hiring decisions for senior-level executives are based on merit, for instance, and yet the percentage of women and people of color in those positions is far lower than their percentage in the population at large, are they really saying that women and people of color don't have as much merit as white men? Perhaps not consciously and certainly without ill intent, but isn't that the takeaway message?

If women and people of color have the same merit as white men, why are their numbers in such short supply in certain companies and certain types of positions?

Within this argument, though, lies an opportunity. For companies that are increasingly struggling to fill certain roles and find that their workforce populations of women and people of color don't represent the populations of available talent, they have an opportunity to close that gap.

BARRIER #3 – Not Casting a Wider Net

To make the situation even more challenging, there's evidence to suggest that women, in particular, may think themselves out of even applying for a job unless they feel they are 100 percent qualified. Author Tara Sophia Mohr was skeptical about findings that had been quoted in "Lean In" and various articles on the topic, so she decided to do some research of her own. She interviewed more than 1,000 men and women to ask: "If you decided not to apply for a job because you didn't meet all the qualifications, why didn't you apply?" She wrote about her findings in a Harvard Business Review article, "Why Women Don't Apply for Jobs Unless They're 100% Qualified."[33]

As indicated in the chart below, women were more likely than men to choose not to even apply for a job if they felt they didn't

---

[32] https://bit.ly/2y8Ehh9

[33] https://bit.ly/1zZzB3B

meet the requirements. The top three barriers cited by women, according to Mohr are "I didn't think they would hire me since I didn't meet the qualifications and I didn't want to waste my time and energy" (40.6 percent), "I didn't think they would hire me since I didn't meet the qualifications and I didn't want to put myself out there if I was likely to fail" (21.6 percent), and "I was following the guidelines about who should apply" (15 percent)—together accounting for about 77 percent of women's reasons for not applying.

Women, says Mohr, are simply more likely to take the written job qualifications more seriously.

Why Didn't You Apply for That Job?

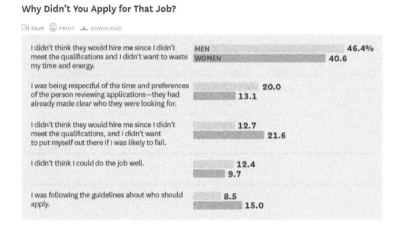

Both women and men tend to take job requirements, on their face, as requirements, rather than attributes that can help people be most successful in a job, suggests Mohr, but women are more likely to fail to act based on fear of failure. Mohr points to three reasons this may be the case:

- In certain work environments, women may need to meet more of the qualifications than their male counterparts.
- Girls are strongly socialized to follow the rules and are rewarded for doing so while in school. "In part, girls' greater success in school (relative to boys) arguably can be attributed to their better rule following," Mohr writes.
- Certifications and degrees have had different impacts for men and women. "The 20th century saw women break into professional life—but only if they had the right training, the right accreditations," says Mohr.

In "Strategies to Increase Workplace Innovation Related to Organizational Performance,"[34] Mansi Pandey with the Jagran College of Arts, Science and Commerce, Kanpur, writes that: "Diversity in the workforce is a goal for most organizations. According to employers, business results affirm the logic behind a heterogeneous workforce. In fact, 75 percent of employers attest that diversity efforts contribute to the bottom line by improving performance and building new leadership. Yet, many admit they do not know how to implement inclusiveness initiatives." Pandey goes on to say that: "Part of the difficulty is that diversity is more than meets the eye. In addition to the visible variations, such as race and gender, it comprises the invisible interests, ideologies and cultural background of what makes each individual just that. It extends across all personal, social, and organizational categories, including age, ethnicity, care-giving responsibility, job type, tenure, and even personal interests." It's not just women and people of color, although that tends to be the focus—inclusion is for *everyone.*"

Winning the War for Talent

In 2018, Michelin North America was recognized by Forbes Magazine as their number one large employer in the United States. The award, says Johnson, "in some ways reflects what we're doing with D&I. The reason I say that is you can't be the number one employer unless your employees feel that they're included, that they're respected—which is one of our core values —and that they really understand the purpose of the company and feel empowered that they can be themselves at work to help deliver on the values and purpose of the company."

At Walmart, says Fan, there is a strong focus on the talent life cycle and ensuring that inclusion is built in throughout the talent life cycle. "We call it 'embedding CDI [culture, diversity and inclusion] into the talent life cycle,'" he says. "We make CDI a dynamic part of total talent strategy. We collaborate with centers of excellence and instill it into four career phases: hire, grow, learn and reward."

A foundational first step in this process is ensuring that job descriptions themselves are inclusive. "Usually the job

---

[34] https://bit.ly/2y98kFv

descriptions come out of talent acquisition areas, and they are not experts in the diversity side of it," says Fan. To combat this, Walmart has internal and external experts review job descriptions to ensure that language is neutral, rather than biased, and inclusive to appeal to a wide range of talent with varying backgrounds.

Once resumes are received, they are reviewed by recruiters to hide names and any other indicators of gender or race. The selection process itself includes a number of decision-makers both when picking whom to interview and when conducting interviews. "Final selection decisions are made by the group and not just one hiring manager," Fan says.

Ensuring inclusion throughout the talent life cycle means that efforts to ensure inclusion and eliminate bias must be in place even after candidates are hired. "Walmart's CDI scorecard incorporates a promotional matrix to help make sure that when we promote our associates, it's done in an unbiased and inclusive way. In addition, diversity and inclusion are also top of mind when we select high-potential associates and when we provide educational and development opportunities. It is not just an afterthought," says Fan.

To ensure shared understanding and open eyes to the implications of unconscious bias that affects everyone, Walmart trained more than 70,000 managers on unconscious bias last year and is planning an unconscious bias 2.0 refresher. The first session, says Fan, focused on raising awareness of the ways that unconscious bias can come into play when making business and people decisions. The next session will be more focused on identifying blind spots and teaching strategies for mitigating unconscious bias.

"Our vision is *Everyone Included*," says Fan. When our associates feel included and valued, everyone wins—the associates are happier and perform at their best and, in return, provide better service to our customers.

It's clear that there are barriers that can negatively impact employers hoping to win the war for talent. A consistent theme among the organizations we've talked to is the importance of inclusion—and how often inclusion isn't occurring at key points in the hiring process, and the overall employee life cycle. Systems have been historically stacked against diverse candidates on a number of levels; by gaining insights into how your hiring, selection and promotion processes may cause candidates to opt out or be overlooked, you can help build a more diverse workforce, which, we know, leads to better employee engagement, retention, and productivity.

5 Diversity Fatigue

It's a real paradox that at a time when the greatest changes are happening in the workforce and emerging markets, a fatigue has set in as far as diversity is concerned. While many organizations are continuing to make efforts to promote diversity strategies, they often come up short.

Let's revisit the concept of diversity fatigue. Many organizations are sick of hearing about how they should or must be more diverse by hiring more women, hiring more people of color, and opening the ranks of upper management to underrepresented groups.

To some extent, these complaints are valid, as organizations have historically used the number of women and people of color at all levels of the organization as a primary diversity approach.

But when the focus is only on representation, diversity fatigue sets in. What lies behind this phenomenon?

- The focus on representation didn't include everyone. Diversity seemed like it was only for women and people of color. By their nature, representation metrics excluded white men, who today still lead over 96 percent of Fortune 500 companies.
- Diversity seemed to be *driven* by representation metrics. And many white men, who bore the brunt of the lack of change, didn't feel included
- Focusing on representation alone did not make the strong business link that was required to make diversity mission critical.
- Diversity was seen as a U.S. phenomenon only and didn't seem relevant globally. Inclusion is a global construct—diversity was seen as a continuation of affirmative action.

While the language of diversity was a way to address a broad range of differences, the focus turned primarily to talent acquisition and development of women and people of color. It came across in comments like, "Get me a list of women or people of color. I need to make that my next hire or promotion."

That's the simple part. For years we've been hiring people through the front door and losing them out the back door. Then the commentary heard is, "They just didn't fit here." Really? It's their fault their voice wasn't heard, and new ideas didn't come forward? Let's stop right here. **If the culture isn't inclusive, you're not going to keep your best talent**—especially when that talent is different from the broader population.

This phenomenon not only shows up with women and people of color, but with other aspects of diversity. For example, it shows up frequently in this scenario: "Let's get some innovative thinkers in here." Accordingly, brilliant, out-of-the-box thinkers are hired. Within a few months, these individuals are pegged as problematic. "They don't know how we do things here. They're not a cultural fit." They even frequently get executive coaches assigned to them to help them better fit in! But this is the crux of the problem, isn't it? **It's the *culture* that must change, not the individual**. The culture must change to allow those who aren't the same (those who are, by definition, diverse) to bring the totality of their brilliance into the workplace, even if their brilliance doesn't fit the mold—in fact, *especially* if their brilliance doesn't fit the mold. That's inclusion!

Inclusion calls us to action. It's not limited to representation metrics as the primary driver. That focus leads organizations into a talent acquisition frenzy. It's not that there's anything wrong with recruiting diverse candidates, but I've seen organizations spend tens of thousands of dollars participating in recruiting events just to, essentially, check a box. Their intent may be noble, but their thinking is limited.

These numbers may reflect diversity, but I'm here to tell you that these numbers are not measures of inclusion…or, more importantly, business impact.

Inclusion is not about counting different categories of employees, yet that is what most organizations tend to do as they focus on inclusion and diversity initiatives. Measures of inclusion go well beyond counting people; they leverage business results.

When organizations wish to increase revenue, they develop growth strategies to help them accomplish that goal. When they hope to reduce costs, they develop meaningful, measurable objectives along with strategies and tactics to help drive down those costs. Yet when organizations address issues related to inclusion and diversity, their metrics (assuming they have them) tend to focus on representation metrics: how many women do we have in leadership positions? How many employees do we have representing certain minority groups?

I'm not saying these organizations should stop counting. Diversity metrics have been and will remain extremely important as part of an overall strategy that links to the bottom line. Yet simply tracking the numbers is a halfhearted effort that only focuses on the population and fails to integrate strengths. It does nothing to address the environment in which people work every day. It does nothing to address what needs to be done to ensure that talent brought into the organization has the expertise and resources to meet business goals.

A company may hire the greatest talent, but if there isn't a culture of inclusion, that talent will move on.

The Drivers of a Quest for Diversity

Historically, the focus on diversity has been driven by political, legal, and moral issues. Diversity gained momentum in the 1960s to level the playing field for people of color and women. It was considered the right thing to do.

Over the last half-century, we have seen increasing gains in workplace diversity starting with President Kennedy's signing of Executive Order 10925 in 1961, when we first saw the term affirmative action. That was over 50 years ago, and it led to the passage of the Civil Rights Act in 1964.

Meanwhile, organizations that embraced diversity work seemed to focus on hiring women and people of color or focused on training. Over time, these good intentions to create a more ethnically and racially diverse workforce began to focus on getting representation and educating people about differences. This has been a numbers game that in many cases lacked a clear business linkage. Corporate America has been spinning its wheels for decades, attempting to influence change by focusing on the numbers, and it hasn't worked.

To date, training has been a primary driver to address diversity awareness needs within organizations. In implementing this training, many organizations have taken a personal, internalized approach. There are academic approaches that determine how biased we are and categorize us as employees as a way of determining organizational readiness.

But where is the business linkage? Where are the resulting behaviors that impact the business identified? How do we hold people accountable?

Learning should be a result of a current state analysis and a component within a business strategy. What are the other training drivers that need to shift within organizations?

- Companies must move from diversity management alone to creating a culture of inclusion.
- Companies must extend learning beyond just senior leaders and implement an enterprise-wide approach with methodology appropriate for all levels of the organization.
- Companies must make the business linkage, including engagement, productivity, innovation, and retention.
- Companies must urge inclusion and diversity training efforts that are more than a dip and done (where training happens every three to seven years but with no accountability or performance plan in between).
- Companies must create a systematic accelerated Learning Over Time® strategy using metrics and accountability.
- Companies must be strategic; inclusion and diversity training efforts must move past awareness and link back to business behaviors in the workplace.
- Companies must measure the transfer of behaviors back to the workplace to ensure the effectiveness of the training.
- Companies must hold people accountable.

Little Progress is Being Made

The evidence of the fatigue shows up in the results. Only 16 companies among the Fortune 500 share detailed demographics on their workforce.[35] Still, these companies represent 800,000 employees and lend a view into how women and people of color are faring in today's workplace. And how are they faring? The answer is - not well.

In 2018, women held 10.6 percent (or 643) of the more than 6,000 board seats in Fortune 500 companies, according to

---

[35] https://for.tn/2scHBGG

Catalyst.[36] Only 3 of the Fortune 500 CEOs are black, according to CNN.[37]

An article in The New York Times by Claire Cain Miller, Kevin Quealy and Margot Sanger-Katz really drives home the statistic about chief executives. The article looks at a number of disparities in industries and professions ranging from finance and law to politics and business. One eye-opening stat we shared previously is that there are fewer women among chief executives of Fortune 500 companies than there are men named John.[38]

Wow! In other words, we still have a long way to go. And, unfortunately, we're losing some ground. In 2018, Indra Nooyi announced her retirement—this will reduce the number of women Fortune 500 CEOs to 23 once she steps down.

"Women remain underrepresented at every level in Corporate America, despite earning more college degrees than men for 30 years and counting," according to McKinsey & Company.[39] People of color are losing out as well.

Consider the disparities in career progression from McKinsey that we discussed previously. Women are disadvantaged at an early point in their careers and struggle to catch up after that. It happens right out of the gate with the very first promotion.

Why, despite so much attention paid to the importance of diversity and inclusion over the past several years, are we still seeing such dismal progress? It's complicated. It has to do with what is an inherently unequal playing field in boardrooms and C-suites around the country. We need to look at the step, behind the step, behind the outcome. When we think about why we keep replicating the same results year over year in Corporate America, we need to think about how talent gets to the table.

---

[36] https://bit.ly/2ynWXZE

[37] https://cnnmon.ie/2RAO4ov

[38] https://nyti.ms/2qVat4l

[39] https://mck.co/2yt54r2

How Talent Gets to the Table

A look at what we're seeing with the Oscars' and the Academy of Motion Picture Arts and Sciences' attempt to add more diversity to the voting ranks can help to illustrate how talent gets to the table. The 2018 annual Oscar awards illustrated, once again, that women and people of color continue to be overlooked for their significant contributions. How can that happen in 2018? It happens several layers back. Historically, members of the Academy of Motion Picture Arts and Sciences have represented a group of industry experts, selected through a very secretive process. Over the past several years, in response to an uproar over the lack of diversity among both nominees and award winners, the Academy has promised to double the number of its minority and female members by 2020. That's a misleading promise that is not as magnanimous as it initially seems and that is also unlikely to have any major impact on the movies, actors, and directors we see honored in future ceremonies.

Why? It's a numbers game.

In 2015, there were 7,000 Academy members. In 2015, the Academy invited 322 new members.[40] In 2016, 683 new members were invited. In 2017, an additional 774 new members were invited. This is all part of a promise to add more diverse faces like Selma star David Oyelowo, Get Out director Jordan Peele, Fame and Ragtime actress Debbie Allen, and others to the organization. The Academy has proudly boasted that "there has been a 331% increase of people of color invited to join the Academy from 2015–2017," according to an article in Variety.[41] The reason that percentage is so high, or course, is because of the dismally small numbers of women and people of color that have historically been part of the group.

Consider this: even if every single one of those new members added over the past three years represented women or people of color, they would represent only 25 percent of the members; of course, they're *not* all women or people of color. At this rate, it will take decades for a meaningful change to occur!

———————————————

[40] https://lat.ms/2yq4d7l

[41] https://bit.ly/2yClvOE

I'm not suggesting that the Academy doesn't have good intentions, just as companies around the country also have good intentions as they strive to build more diverse, and more inclusive, workplaces. What I *am* suggesting, though, is that the issue is more complex than it appears on the surface. We need to take a look at the step, behind the step, behind the outcome.

Let's consider how people get selected to be in the Academy. They must have experience in the motion picture industry. Because white men have, historically, held those positions in numbers disproportionate to white women and people of color, even among actors, they're statistically more likely to be part of the field of potential candidates.

It's the same thing that we see in workplace settings, and it reminds me of organizations we've worked with that had the number of years of experience as part of their core criteria. Whether it was financial or sports entertainment, the criteria of five to 10-plus years of experience was a barrier. Women and people of color were unintentionally disqualified. Once organizations recognized the unequal footing these criteria resulted in, they changed the criteria to focus on the specific competencies people needed to succeed in this role. They also shifted to a new focus on potential, rather than experience, as the reason for someone being promotable.

So, going back to the Oscars, a critical competency that Academy members must have to address the need for a more multicultural perspective is having that multicultural perspective. When that becomes "the" core competency, *then* we'll start to level the playing field.

A Different Experience for Women and People of Color

A focus on generational differences can be insightful, but it masks more pervasive issues related to diversity, inclusion, and success in the workplace. What we are finding in our work, and what is supported in the literature, is that women and people of color, regardless of generation, are hindered in their ability to achieve top roles in most organizations. Worse, many leave to seek opportunities elsewhere, resulting in the loss of talent for the very organizations that lament their ability to *find* good talent. Far too often, they've *found* it; they just aren't doing enough to *retain* it!

Women's workforce participation rates have increased in just about every country around the world since 2000—except the United States—according to research from the Organization for Economic Cooperation and Development.[42]

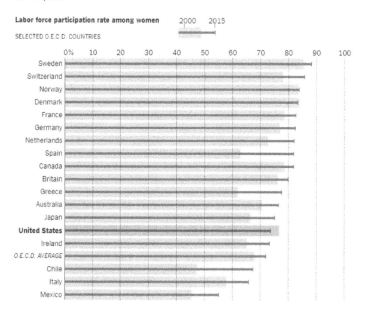

Women in the Work Force

Women's participation in the labor force has increased since 2000 in almost every major country in the Organization for Economic Cooperation and Development. The United States is one of the few exceptions.

Source: Analysis of data from the Organization for Economic Cooperation and Development by John Coglianese, Harvard University

By The New York Times

Why? There's some evidence to suggest that women, even girls, may simply give up. A study in Science, reported in Fortune,[43] indicates that girls as young as 6 believe that boys (men) are simply naturally smarter than they are. The study was conducted among 400 children, aged 5 to 7. As the study's authors pointed out: "These stereotypes discourage women's pursuit of many

---

[42] https://nyti.ms/2jWLHOn

[43] https://for.tn/2kbLION

prestigious careers; that is, women are underrepresented in fields whose members cherish brilliance."

The situation is not that dissimilar when considering self-perceptions of people of color. While the same data isn't available for people of color, the following chart shows the disparity in terms of executive ethnic diversity and the percentage of the population who are minorities. We have a minority population of 39 percent—yet boards of directors and executive teams are comprised of only 15 and 12 percent minority members, respectively. That's a disparity that is difficult to justify. It reflects some real gaps in terms of not only recruiting, but also retaining people of color through inclusive leadership.

Executive ethnic diversity relative to population

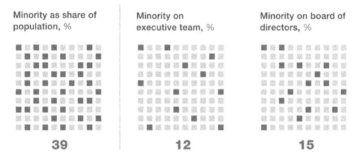

Minority as share of population, %	Minority on executive team, %	Minority on board of directors, %
39	**12**	**15**

Note: The definition of "ethnic minority" varies by country, based on the local understanding of which groups have been historically underrepresented politically or in business. In South Africa, minority refers to black Africans. In the United States, it refers to black or African Americans, Hispanics or Latinos, Asians or Pacific Islanders, Native Americans, anyone of mixed race, or other nonwhite ethnicities. In the United Kingdom, it includes everyone excluding whites or white British. In Singapore, we have only included people of Malay decent.

Source: Government of Singapore; UK Office of National Statistics; US Census Bureau; McKinsey analysis

McKinsey&Company

The Evidence is Overwhelming

In 2018, in the 25 states with the highest number of Latinas working full time, Latinas earned 42–61 cents for every dollar paid to white, non-Hispanic men, according to the National Partnership for Women & Families.[44] Yet, while we continue to see disparities based on race, we are seeing signs of progress in statistics that show us more women than men are now graduating and getting college degrees, master's degrees, and doctorates.

---

[44] https://bit.ly/1E9LLj1

These may be signs of progress, but economic disparities are greater than ever, and a far greater number of people feel disenfranchised. The economic gap continues to grow, and the middle class is disappearing. It now takes two incomes for young people to even approach the lifestyles their parents had. This goes beyond race and gender.

It's not that race and gender aren't still important, but in today's world of the new business normal, the conversations have become much more complex and nuanced. InclusionINC, my consulting firm, has created assessments to determine where the breakdowns occur, what stands in the way of being fully engaged, and what it takes to ensure employees feel included and can be most innovative and productive. From data collected from this assessment work with more than 300,000 U.S. employees across multiple industries, primarily in the corporate environment, I have found that breakdowns occur primarily because of five key factors:

1. This is the first time in U.S. history in which we have five generations in the workplace.
2. Cross-cultural issues are emerging whether you're dealing with a global colleague or someone from your own office.
3. Not all organizations fully understand that employee engagement and productivity are driven by everyone's contribution to the business.
4. Not all organizations have the ability to drive innovation by effectively including all perspectives.
5. Technology has significantly changed how individuals communicate; inclusive communication is becoming even more critically important for innovation.

Many businesses are ill-prepared to recognize, let alone address, these factors because of the complexities involved.

Inclusion Makes Sound Business Sense

It's our mantra: inclusion is a strategic and business imperative. But, while we have led the pack in this work since our inception more than a decade ago, we're no longer alone in our thinking. That's a very good thing! As Walmart's Fan says, a strategic focus on diversity and inclusion can lead to "more strength in marketplace presence, enhanced customer satisfaction and can build organizational capacity and leadership excellence." Inclusion also drives innovation, he says, which is critical in today's fast-changing world. "For us, diversity and inclusion, and our corporate culture, play an essential role for us to win in this digital age."

Ken Barrett's experience also supports the notion that the quest for inclusion must be framed from a business perspective. When Barrett first assumed the position of Chief Diversity Officer at General Motors (GM), he says then-chairman and CEO Dan Akerson told him: "We're supportive of diversity and inclusion here at General Motors, but it's critical that you really understand the business. If you're not able to clearly articulate the business impact of what you're doing, then it's not going to resonate with the folks inside the company." Barrett says he took that advice to heart. He says it has served him well in his role and has helped him achieve some significant and measurable successes.

Sodexo has done research into the impact of diversity in leadership, says Harris. For instance, she says: "We've done studies around gender balance and have found that there's a sweet spot of having 40–60 percent of men and women in leadership, where there is greater performance, engagement, and better business outcomes." Because of that, she says, "it has changed the conversation a bit to get people really engaged and understanding what's in it for them on a business level and how we can benefit from a diverse workforce."

The Call to Action

Today, we need to do something different. We need to move from a focus on diversity to a focus on inclusion and diversity or, simply, a focus on inclusion. Not because it's the right thing to do but because it is a business imperative. The war for talent is now! Businesses that wish to succeed in an environment facing such seismic shifts must focus on strategies designed to attract, retain, and generate input and innovative ideas from a changing, but also shrinking, talent base.

Why aren't we seeing sweeping changes at organizations around the country as they actively seek to meld the concepts of knowledge and manual workers? Because, despite the oft-stated belief that employees are our most valuable asset, most companies are still tied to the old command-and-control traditions that may have served them in decades past but are woefully inadequate to serve them in the world they exist in today. As Marshall Goldsmith profoundly proclaimed in his popular book by the same title, "What got you here won't get you there."

IT'S ABOUT BUSINESS

6 Inclusion is the Solution to Employee Engagement and Retention

Inclusion drives engagement and retention. If you want your top employees to stay with you—and who doesn't—they need to know their value, have opportunities to contribute and recognize that their managers, and the organization as a whole, are committed to their growth and development. In fact, according to Employee Benefit News, next to paid family leave (58 percent) and flexible/remote work options (55 percent), employees value professional development (39 percent). They cite research from Kaplan Financial, which indicates that when employers offer professional development, they benefit through "increased retention, easier succession planning and greater efficiency."[45]

The inclusive companies we spoke with know this.

At GM, says Barrett, Employee Resource Groups (ERGs) provide opportunities for experiences that can lead to future leadership roles. "There's a leadership structure in each one of these ERGs, so we've had multiple opportunities for employees who may not be managers or executives in their particular functions today to be able to take on leadership responsibilities inside the ERG." This has, he says, "been an indicator for us of those people that really are rising stars in the organization."

Building and nurturing a pipeline of diverse talent to rise into leadership ranks and key positions has been an area of challenge for Mortenson, says Weiss, because their employee population has been predominantly white men. But she says: "I have seen us make progress in selecting women and people of color for high-profile projects, which is pretty exciting." While she says there is no "grand plan," she adds: "We're trying to ensure that our leaders are pushing and growing their people as appropriate." It will, she says, be a continued area of focus in the future.

The automotive industry is another that has, historically, been made up of employees—and leaders—who are predominantly white males. Breaking that trend requires a focus on not only hiring diverse talent but also finding ways to help them make their way to the top echelons of the organization. That's exactly

---

[45] https://bit.ly/2PxCKbc

what GM has done. "I think we're like one of three companies in the Fortune 500 to have both a woman as a CEO and a CFO," says Barrett. "I think it's a testament to our focus on this over time." That focus starts in the very early stages of an employee's career. Barrett points to Alicia Boler Davis, GM's executive Vice President of Global Manufacturing and an African American woman, as one prime example.

Boler Davis, an engineer, started with GM as an intern while still in high school; she then went to a STEM camp that GM sponsored. Later, she attended Northwestern and graduated as a chemical engineer. She is, says Barrett, "a very prominent woman in the organization, who sits on the senior leadership team and has been able to move all the way through all the levels in the company to get to the top in manufacturing. She, arguably, runs the largest manufacturing job in the world."

This is why inclusion is the solution for employee engagement and retention.

Inclusion isn't just an HR or feel-good topic. It impacts business results. A recent McKinsey report "Delivering Through Diversity"[46] offers some compelling evidence for the importance of diversity and inclusion:

- "Companies in the top-quartile for gender diversity on their executive teams were 21% more likely to have above-average profitability than companies in the fourth quartile. For ethnic/cultural diversity, top-quartile companies were 33% more likely to outperform on profitability."
- "Companies in the top-quartile for gender diversity on executive teams were 21% more likely to outperform their national industry median on EBIT margin and 27% on EP margin."
- "Companies with the most ethnically/culturally diverse boards worldwide are 43% more likely to experience higher profits."[47]

So, how do you get from here to there?

---

[46] https://mck.co/2wrk8og

[47] https://mck.co/2ynN8uW

Nurturing a Culture of Inclusion

The answer is simple: a workplace culture of inclusion. You get there by fostering a culture of inclusion from the top of the organization down through all levels and across all locations.

Inclusion provides key insights and behaviors that ensure connectivity to the complexity of the current global market. Inclusion is about encouraging people to share their best ideas. Inclusion means getting people to participate in reaching the best outcome for the organization. Inclusion is about getting everyone in the game to ensure their voices are heard to improve overall business success. Inclusion is the best practical solution for employee engagement.

Why has employee engagement become such a huge matter, and how does inclusion impact it? Let's start with defining employee engagement, which measures the level of connection employees feel toward their employer as demonstrated by their willingness and ability to help their company succeed, largely by providing discretionary effort on a sustained basis.

Inclusion, as we further explain in chapter 9, is an action word that means taking everyone's voice and talents into account. It means being open to a variety of ideas, knowledge, perspectives, approaches, and styles. It means everyone is allowed to bring their best to the workplace to maximize business success.

Today, inclusion and employee engagement are inexorably linked because most employees create value through the synergy that results from a confluence of ideas and information.

That synergy is "absolutely critical for us," says Barrett of GM. "The way we talk about diversity and inclusion at GM is really all the different traits and attributes that people bring to bear. What we want to do is empower people."

Inclusive organizations recognize that they need input from everyone to help drive business decisions and productivity. Frontline staff as well as C-suite leaders have knowledge to share; your most recent hires and people of all levels and roles in your organization provide valid perspectives to improve business processes and results.

Even if your business is based in the U.S., you're not just competing with U.S. companies today. Everything is global—your employees, your markets, and your competition. Hearing and integrating ideas from all your employees is a key driver for success in this new global business normal.

It's not just about having diverse talent; it's about creating a culture of inclusion to harness the way diverse teams work together.

Inclusion means seeking out and listening to *all* voices and inputs.

Importantly, points out BASF's Rossman, "inclusion is not a zero-sum game, where if one group wins another group loses—or where one group of employees is pitted against another." All voices matter, and there is value to assembling diverse voices that bring new perspectives and viewpoints to the discussion. "We know we come up with stronger ideas when they are drawn from a truly diverse and inclusive population that feels empowered and included to share those thoughts and ideas and anticipate and meet market needs in new ways."

Organizations bring in more revenue when they are appropriately focused on meeting the needs of customers, whoever and wherever they are. They bring in more revenue and contain costs when they are fully engaged with their stakeholders - this leads to creative and innovative solutions from their employees that meet customer needs and changing demands.

Engagement is critical for today's companies—more so than ever before as the unemployment rate continues to fall and companies find themselves competing for talent, even in previously easy-to-fill roles. An inclusive culture, says Harris, "is a significant driver of engagement which results in improved performance and productivity". At Sodexo, she says, they've been able to tie their inclusive culture back to engagement as one of the top two drivers. "We're a very global institution—we have 33,000 locations and operate in over 80 countries—a competitive workforce is critical to support and proactively address the needs of our globally diverse marketplace." Mirroring the diversity of their customer base, she says, "is critical to the growth and success of our business."

Clearly, your company's bottom line will benefit by generating new ideas and capitalizing on opportunities for innovation. Unfortunately, too many organizations spend too little time working on creating sustainable, engaging work environments in which people can participate.

Tapping Into the Diverse Talent Market

At Mortenson, says Weiss, the recognition that the company needed to expand diversity to bring in new voices and new perspectives led to a focus on its recruitment practices. "We asked recruiters to think about, and talk a lot about, where they were doing their outreach and to report back every month to be sure we could find new sources of recruitment."

Mortenson was intentional about this outreach. "We were pretty specific about what this meant to us," says Weiss. When looking at candidate pools, she says, "we didn't just want one person different from the others, but at least two - having two levels the playing field and makes the hiring of someone who is different from you more likely. We really focused hard on making sure we provided a diverse slate of candidates."

That intentional approach tied to metrics and accountability is critical. But, as we know, it's not just about *recruiting* a diverse talent pool. Once recruited, we must make sure these recruits feel included, or we risk losing them and their ideas.

That's been a focus of Rossman's work at BASF. She stresses the importance of "being as intentional and deliberate around inclusion as we are around diversity." About six years ago, she says, the company established a dashboard to track retention, including a focus on recent joiners. "We were looking at our hiring patterns and we also wanted to look more deeply at who stays with us. Retention helps us move beyond traditional diversity metrics to better understand retention and engagement."

Based on their analysis, BASF has become very intentional about finding ways to engage employees—new and long tenured —through *intentional* inclusion. This resulted in one very impactful shift in perspective—a move away from the idea that everyone needs to be treated the same. "For very good reasons, I think many of our leaders felt that a badge of courage was 'I don't see differences, I treat everyone the same.' While that came from a good place, what it showed us is that it's not the best way to bring out the best in your team. How can we look deeper at how our differences form the best ways we work?" BASF has utilized Insights Discovery, a program based on the psychology of Carl Jung, to help teams evaluate their different thought processes and to encourage discussions that clarify the different lenses diverse employees look through.

BASF has also worked hard to raise awareness of unconscious bias. At BASF, says Rossman, a lot of work has been done around unconscious bias and helping leaders uncover their own unconscious biases. But she says: "Just knowing about our unconscious biases is only the very first step. It's what are we doing about them; how are we compensating for them?" BASF, she says, is a science-based, data-driven organization, so metrics helped the company uncover areas where unconscious bias may have been at work. "We really started measuring things like 'Where are you drawing your talent from—are you always looking at the same sources? What is your mix of internal and external talent?' We're really trying to change the conversations to say, 'what differences does this person bring to our teams?' It's really that age-old idea that if we're all thinking alike, someone isn't thinking."

In doing this, says Rossman, BASF was able to address certain behaviors that may have been contributing to unconscious bias in the selection processes. "We sat with our teams and looked at the cumulative impact of their hiring decisions to see how we can work together to make sure we truly are selecting the best talent from across the North American market. Our efforts are all about selecting the best person for the role, and ensuring we are selecting talent from across all components of a very diverse and competitive talent market."

Another critical area of focus has been around the idea of hiring for fit, says Rossman, and questioning, "Am I hiring for those who are different, who do not simply multiply the very same strengths we already have but bring in new perspectives?" This approach, she says, "will help us distinguish ourselves in new ways in the market."

InclusionINC's Global Inclusion Index™

One of the most difficult things in this area of work is practically differentiating between diversity and inclusion. Diversity is seen as easier because it's typically measuring representation metrics. Inclusion is harder because you have to *do* something to be inclusive. Measuring a culture of inclusion is very similar to measuring great leadership. It's critically important and can be seen in how someone interacts with others—their behaviors, skills, and competencies.

From the beginning of our inclusion work we have asked, "What does it look like to create a culture of inclusion? What do I do? What are inclusion behaviors?" We asked those questions in our inclusion and diversity current state analyses (customized web-based surveys, focus groups, and interviews that we conducted with employees in client locations). We explored answers to questions like: When do you feel most included? When do you feel most excluded?

Interestingly enough, the same behaviors kept showing up over and over again. We were able to validate inclusion behaviors throughout the U.S. with over 300,000 cross-industry employees at all levels within their organizations. We realized, though, that the majority of our work had been within the U.S. We needed global validation. To that end, in 2013 we partnered with the Cox Executive Education Department and Dr. Miguel Quiñones to create the Global Inclusion Index™ (G2I) to measure 12 inclusion behaviors in a global environment. Those behaviors were then cross-referenced with return on investment (ROI) questions (self-reported retention, engagement, productivity, and innovation questions). The G2I is used to establish a baseline of metrics on inclusion, by site or by business unit/region, when conducted on an enterprise basis. Disparities between behavior importance and frequency, and also across specific groups, were identified as issue indicators.

Here are the stunning results of that work:

- An increase of 25 percent in employee likelihood of being motivated by their jobs
- A reduction of 15 percent in the number of employees likely to leave within the next year
- An increase of 12 percent in likelihood of employees to share ideas and to think of ways to improve the workplace
- An increase of 5 percent in employees likely to report being productive

These are results that really make a difference to your employees and to your bottom line. Yes, it pays to be inclusive.

Toward Belonging

A term that has started to show up in this work is belonging. From a general perspective, belonging is not a new concept. In fact, it's one component of Maslow's famous hierarchy of needs. It's one of our deepest human needs.

From InclusionINC's perspective, belonging is what you personally feel from being included. I can demonstrate inclusion behaviors; I can show that I'm an inclusive leader by how I interact—but I can't make someone belong. From an individual perspective, you know whether you feel like you belong, *and* you may have very specific ways you want to be interacted with to make you feel like you belong. For example, diverse staff members who don't feel like they're a cultural fit, don't feel like their input is sought or valued, and don't feel like their contributions make a meaningful difference won't feel the sense of belonging that leads to long-term tenure, loyalty, and, from the employer's standpoint, retention of top talent.

Belonging is the result of a culture of inclusion and the next logical focus for companies that have worked to create an inclusive culture.

But who defines belonging? Is it senior leadership, HR, or direct managers and supervisors? No. Only employees themselves can determine whether they feel that they belong. Too often they don't feel like they belong, and, when they don't, they're likely to do one of two things: resign in place or look for options elsewhere.

Breaking down walls can help boost feelings of belonging, says Fan with Walmart. The concept of "insiders and outsiders," he says, is what we focus on addressing by promoting open-mindedness.

The concept of belonging is the next phase for many companies that are well along their diversity and inclusion journey.

Cultivating Inclusion Behaviors

To build a foundation for an inclusive culture, you must first cultivate inclusion behaviors across the board. That, of course, can seem like a daunting task. But, before you start to panic, understand that there are some relatively simple ways to engage your diverse workforce:

- Share your strategy with your employees. Let's say you're worried about increasing competition and the emergence of new technology and markets that might make your products obsolete. Have you told your employees, or do you figure they just need to punch in and punch out at the right time and work their part of the assembly line? Do you think, "What could they possibly have to offer me?" If so, your thinking is wrong. Sharing your strategy with employees not only gives them perspective about how their efforts fit into the big picture and drives organizational success but also increases the odds that they will share their unique insights and ideas with you.
- Ask for their input. Include them! If you rely entirely on a handful of managers and top executives to come up with great new ideas, you're missing out on the brainpower of the majority of your workplace. When making hiring decisions, most employers look for employees who are creative, intelligent, and insightful. Why hire people like that if you aren't going to ask for their input? These are the people on the ground, the ones who will implement any new strategy your organization pursues, the ones selling your products and services to your customers, and the ones who have seen firsthand what works and what doesn't.
- Listen and evaluate the idea, not the person presenting it. What could that 21-year-old business graduate possibly know about improving productivity or product quality? What could that 62-year-old possibly know about technology? You might be surprised. Similarly, as your markets and customer base become more diverse, it is increasingly important to get input from all your employees. Don't you think your Hispanic employees might have some insights into the tastes of their friends, families, and communities? When you put up barriers in your mind as to the value of the input and opinions that

employees have to offer, you're being exclusive. Your employees lose out, and so do you!

- Act on what you determine to be the best course of action. You can't implement everyone's suggestions, and that's okay. Inclusion is first and foremost about making sure everyone gets a chance to be heard, even if their ideas aren't always used.
- Provide feedback to your employees about why you did or did not act on their suggestions. Again, it's impossible and impractical to use everyone's suggestions, but your employees might think their ideas were particularly useful and may be confused if they aren't implemented. It's important to let them know specifically why one path was taken and not another. This will reassure employees that their ideas were truly considered and not passed over. Additionally, this will benefit your organization by improving future input. If any employee's input is particularly helpful, let them know specifically how it contributed to the final decision and how it will help the company.
- Thank your employees for being willing to contribute. Think about times when you've contributed something to a brainstorming session or strategic planning effort. Did you feel you received recognition or appreciation for your contribution? Too often, the answer is no. Simply stopping at an employee's desk to take a few seconds to personally thank them can go a long way toward making them feel included and eager to contribute in the future. Let them know that even if their ideas aren't being used this time around, you feel they have a lot to offer, and you look forward to getting their input in the future

Hopefully you've noticed an important three-part theme resonating in all these suggestions: ask, listen, and respond with rationale. The key to creating an inclusive workplace is often as simple as being more effective at communicating. Even the most well meaning workplace can seem exclusionary if there is poor communication. Taking the extra time to share new strategies with employees and simply asking what they think can go a long way toward making employees feel valued and engaged. And, who knows, you might learn a thing or two in the process!

How a Culture of Inclusion Impacts Retention

Employers have increasingly been unable to demonstrate loyalty to their workers. Employees have abandoned loyalty in return. While job-hopping used to be considered a bad thing by the old guard, those who have multiple experiences at multiple companies are often highly valued today for their breadth of knowledge, their agility, and their broad insights. But while your biotechnology firm might be eager to hire a thirty-something with experience at four major competitors over the course of a brief career, you're likely not so eager to have your competitors picking off your bright staff members. With them, you'd likely want to see a longer tenure than two years.

Yet recruitment is only part of the equation. If as the CEO of an organization I'm harping about how we don't hire enough women and people of color but I'm not linking that recruitment strategy to the business, these efforts are not going to work. I may be able to recruit from specific groups, but will I be able to keep those I hire? Or will I ultimately be forced to conclude that they just didn't work out?

At Walmart, says Fan, D&I is considered through three different lenses: business, the employee proposition, and customers. In all three areas, a focus on inclusion drives positive outcomes. From the employee standpoint, those outcomes are strongly tied to high engagement and talent retention, he says. The investment in inclusion also strengthens the organization's brand. "Through that enhanced brand reputation, we will be able to attract, develop, and retain not only just diverse talent, but talent as a whole. From the customer perspective, our inclusive service and advocacy influences our customers' selection of Walmart as a retailer of choice."

To move toward the creation of a culture of inclusion that will have meaningful and measurable impacts on retention, companies need to:

- Move past compliance as motivation
- Link their efforts to the business plan
- Focus on the bottom line
- Emphasize inclusion as a culture change
- Focus on the value of each individual
- View employees as assets (i.e., intellectual capital)

Inclusion is about taking action to ensure everyone's voice is heard—because that's what will drive business performance. Everyone means everyone. Yes, it means women and people of color, but it also means men and Caucasians. It means employees who are Republicans and employees who are Democrats, as well as employees who are Muslim, Christian, and Atheist. It means employees who are traditionalists (those born between 1900–1945) and employees who represent Gen Y.

Don't you long for the good old days, when things were simpler and people stayed forever? According to the U.S. Bureau of Labor Statistics, the median job tenure for workers aged 55 to 64 was ten years in 2010. That's more than three times the median job tenure for workers aged 25 to 34, which was 3.1 years. In fact, Experience, Inc. reported in 2008 that 70 percent of Gen Y leaves their first job within two years.

Turnover represents real costs to businesses. Ending an existing employment relationship, finding a replacement, and training that replacement can be a huge drain on your organization. Employee retention is essential for keeping your best and brightest, for keeping your HR costs down, and for minimizing knowledge loss.

Retention in the Ever-Changing Workplace

Today we have five generations in the workplace. This poses a unique issue for retaining your best talent. The key to keeping the best of the best in each generation is to understand the differences and strengths each generation brings to the table. If you understand what makes each generation feel engaged and included, you can be a successful leader of your multigenerational workforce. Generations differ in the way they communicate, in how they view their work, in how they receive feedback, and in what techniques they use to accomplish tasks. Here are some tips to help bridge the generational divide:

- Value diversity of thought
- Know whom you're talking to
- Learn to accept and appreciate everyone's perspective
- Discuss expectations right away
- Make everyone feel included
- Don't be put off by overt ambition
- Keep up with technology

The workforce is also more culturally diverse than ever before. Both on the local and global level, cultural differences can create conflicts in the workplace and lead to retention issues. Depending on their culture, employers and employees alike may have very different perceptions of time, feedback styles, hierarchies, and many other everyday business tasks. Being aware of cultural differences and seeing those differences as strengths can help you retain the culturally diverse workforce that can give you an advantage over your competitors.

As BASF has worked hard to improve diversity in recruiting and selection efforts, its dashboards help ensure the focus remains broad to leverage the diverse North American talent pool. Now, says Rossman, "we're taking a deeper look at retention—who are we retaining? How are we making sure we're connecting with employees—those with high experience levels, those early in their careers, and everyone in between?"

Using Employee Resource Groups Strategically

Creating Employee Resource Groups (ERGs)—also known as Business Resource Groups (BRGs), Employee Networks, or Affinity Groups—can help make your diverse workforce feel more included. Such groups also allow individuals to share their experiences with others who may be having similar experiences to aid in achieving key business objectives.

That last part—"aid in achieving key business objectives"—is critical. ERGs aren't, or shouldn't be, simply social clubs for people with similar characteristics to get together to share stories. They should be strategically designed to drive business goals and objectives.

For example, if your organization is trying to tap into the Chinese market, your Asian Business Resource Group should be included in that discussion, as these individuals have a unique perspective that can help identify the culture and demands of that particular market. Now you not only have the competitive advantage over your competitors who have a room full of Americans trying to decide what the Chinese market might want but also have made your employees feel like they truly belong at your organization by making this contribution.

At Michelin, Herb Johnson says, Business Resource Groups have grown from three focused on women and people of color to ten, now including LGBTQ employees and the most recent group focused on faiths and beliefs and people of all abilities. At Michelin, inclusion truly is for everyone. "When people feel like they're included, it makes all the difference in the world," says Johnson. "We may not have the hard numbers, but anecdotally we know we're headed in the right direction."

Importantly, Johnson notes, these groups should be viewed not as social gatherings but more like lunch and learns—an opportunity to talk about different cultures and grow to respect differences.

Michelin's Business Resource Groups are integral to the company's D&I strategy and play a key role in developing a culture where everyone is free to bring their whole and authentic selves to work each day, says Johnson. "We want all employees to feel welcome, included and purposeful. We want to attract top talent with unique perspectives that will help us solve not only our business challenges, but also the mobility challenges impacting people around the world."

At Sodexo, says Harris, ERBGs provide opportunities for employees to gain leadership experience and to interact with Sodexo leaders. Most of Sodexo's ERBGs are headed by either a director or VP-level employee. The employee lead sets strategy and works with one, or more, senior leaders who serve as executive sponsors and, says Harris: "are very involved in helping define and support the group's business plan to address specific goals and objectives related to their constituencies." This, she says, provides employees with "great senior leadership visibility in taking on these national assignments and driving the work across the U.S. and down into local chapters across the nation."

GM is also strategically using its 11 ERGs—with more than 75 chapters—to focus on talent and market business objectives. Each ERG has a business plan that's tied to four areas of focus:

- Talent acquisition—making sure the group is bringing more of their represented constituency into the workplace
- Talent development—ensuring that career development opportunities (e.g., mentorships, sponsorships, etc.) exist

to help these constituencies grow and develop within the organization
- Community outreach—ERGs are charged with connecting with their constituencies outside the organization. This provides a clear tie back to the business case, says Barrett of GM—"Are you helping us to sell cars?" ERG members are expected to be vehicle advocates who can go after conquest sales in their constituencies for GM products.
- Ethnic and women share of brand—"We have actual measures to be able to say, 'are we at our market share' for these particular constituencies and then what do we need to do for targeted advertising, marketing and engagement to actually bring those customers into the fold," says Barrett.

It doesn't get more business focused than that. When ERGs are business-centric and purpose-driven, they get meaningful results that help grow both the business and ERG members' careers. ERG members feel their voices are heard and they feel valued. That's inclusion!

Retaining GEN Y . . . Really!

Let's get a couple things on the table right now. Gen Y is never going to grow up to be like the Baby Boomers. They are already grown up! Whereas Baby Boomers were likely to stay with one company for years and sometimes for entire careers, Gen Y (as dynamic and as creative as they are) is a far less loyal cohort. This generation knows it can easily transition between jobs and careers, and Gen Y places a huge value on work-life balance. These folks don't want to be forced to abandon time with family and friends for a career. They work to live, rather than live to work, and they will shop around until they find a job that allows them to do just that. With a rebounding economy, Gen Y (and Gen Z) now have choices about where to work because there aren't quite enough of them to fill the jobs that are now available.

What will help to make these new entrants to the workforce choose you? You may be surprised. According to research from Department26, reported by Ladders, what's most important to Millennials when they get a new job is being in a role they're passionate about (44 percent), topping money which comes in at 42 percent. "'The Millennials we surveyed and interviewed rated 'passion' as a top priority because purpose is more important to this generation than the previous two,' Miki Reilly-Howe, Managing Director of Department26, told Ladders."[48]

Talent Economy points to 2016 research from Cone Communications, which revealed that:

- 75 percent of Millennials would take a pay cut to work for a socially responsible company.
- 76 percent of Millennials consider a company's social and environmental commitments before deciding where to work.
- 64 percent of Millennials won't take a job if a potential employer doesn't have strong corporate responsibility practices.[49]

Millennials also want to be heard.

Research by Gallup reveals that, even more than other generations, Gen Y wants to meet regularly with their managers —when they do, they're more engaged.[50] Unfortunately, this generation is also the *least engaged*. Only 29 percent of Millennials are engaged, according to Gallup's research; another 16 percent are actively disengaged. That means, says Gallup's report that "they are more or less out to do damage to their company." Another 55 percent are somewhere in the middle— simply not engaged. They're not, necessarily, looking for new jobs, but "they feel indifferent about their job and company."

The research suggests one readily available recourse—connect with your employees! "Forty-four percent of Millennials who report that their manager holds regular meetings with them are engaged—contrasting sharply with the 20 percent of engaged Millennials who do not agree that their manager meets with them regularly," says the Gallup report. The report goes on to indicate that this finding is similar to older generations: "43 percent of non-Millennials who report their manager holds regular meetings with them are engaged."

---

[48] https://bit.ly/2Ev4hUM

[49] https://bit.ly/2Plc5yc

[50] https://bit.ly/2y76Ili

Those meetings provide an opportunity not only for feedback from managers but also for input to managers. This is a generation that wants their voices heard—and they want to be heard now! "Gen Ys want to be valued, feel their voice is heard and also look for public recognition of their achievements," Alec Marsh writes in "What Does Gen Y Want?"[51]

If you're a Boomer reading this, you're no doubt thinking life's not fair. You're right. Members of Gen Y simply don't have to do what you did to get ahead. Step back and learn something from them. Gen Y is bringing something to the workplace that no other generation has before. This generation has the ability to turn business on its head. They, in fact, are in a position of interviewing potential employers more than these employers interviewing them.

Corporate America will either embrace this changing dynamic or it won't, and embracing this dynamic means embracing inclusion, which is critical to retaining Gen Y employees.

Talent as a Value Proposition

GM's value propositions have a dual focus on talent and market. From a talent standpoint, Barrett says, the company's ERGs play an important role in helping to source talent—one of each group's measurable goals is bringing diverse new talent to the organization.

Barrett works to ensure that GM's ERG efforts also are aligned with any career development programs at the company. Beyond ERGs, other initiatives may focus on critical areas of need—for instance, he says, growing the number of women in manufacturing positions. "We have a lot of people in manufacturing, and we want to be able to make sure that our women employees are successful in manufacturing, so we have a boot camp where we accelerate their growth in that particular area."

Another area of focus has been LGBTQ. Pride Month, he says, gets a lot of attention at GM, and the attention is growing. "About six years ago when we were trying to showcase our LGBTQ population, we had about three locations across the U.S.

---

[51] https://bit.ly/2ylAXi8

that flew the rainbow flag. I'm definitely inspired by the fact that this year, we had 74 different installations that were flying the rainbow flag or doing rainbow coloring." He points to Cadillac as one example.

Despite some concerted focus on women and the LGBTQ community, though, Barrett with GM, stresses the importance of an ongoing, overall approach tied to a high-level organizational strategy—throughout the year and not just during seasonal observations like Pride Month. Understanding which talent segments are underrepresented, though, is an important means of framing strategy and the tactics designed to achieve goals and objectives.

Another area of focus at GM is talent development, one of their four key areas of focus, to ensure that specific subsets of talent are ready to move into new roles as they emerge. To support these efforts, "there are some pretty robust mentoring circles," Barrett says, including reverse mentoring. "We try to make sure we impact the talent pipeline throughout and make sure that, as we move up from new hire all the way up to executive and senior executive, we have a robust pipeline throughout and that the development of that is in place."

Today's employees, particularly Generation Y, know how valuable they are. They know they have great ideas and viewpoints to share, and they want to be heard. Keeping the decision-making process in the hands of a few top executives shut away in their ivory towers will not fly with employees anymore. An old dentists' adage says, "Ignore your teeth, and they'll go away." The same can be said about employees in today's workforce. Employees who feel like their opinions aren't included in the discussion will simply transition to more inclusive work environments, possibly with one of your competitors.

When I wrote the first edition of this book, employers were growing complacent about their ability to keep employees on board during a very tight economy. But things are changing and changing rapidly. An extensive survey conducted by Mental Health America and The Faas Foundation from 2015-2017, "Mind the Workplace," indicated that 71 percent of respondents were "actively looking for new job opportunities" or had the idea on their mind "always, often or sometimes."[52]

The economy has been continuing an uphill climb since these results were released, giving employees increasingly more options to pursue opportunities elsewhere.

If your company already has a strong culture of inclusion, you might not need to worry too much about that figure. If you aren't a particularly inclusive company, you should be very afraid. Your employees might already be plotting their escape from what they see as a dead-end environment in which they don't feel appreciated.

A Huffington Post article reports that, according to Josh Bersin of Deloitte, "the cost of losing an employee can range from tens of thousands of dollars to 1.5–2.0x the employee's annual salary." There is a wide range of factors that impact these costs: "hiring, onboarding, training, ramp time to peak productivity, the loss of engagement from others due to high turnover, higher business error rates, and general culture impacts."[53] The article provides a link to a spreadsheet that can help you calculate the potential impact of churn on your organization.

If you want to avoid these costs, and, of course, you do, here are some strategies to consider:

1. Build the bridge between differences. Make room for Gen Y. Knowledge workers are techno savvy and they want to have more of a say and to move up faster. Have them work with Baby Boomers or Traditionalists in a reverse mentoring way that has twofold benefits: Boomers or Traditionalists can teach Gen Y about the organization while Gen Y can help Boomers/ Traditionalists keep up on their technology skills.
2. Determine who your keepers are. Who are the best and brightest? Challenge yourself to go beyond those who have traditionally been in key positions in the past.
3. Remember that today's talent in all generations is highly skilled and adept at solving complex business problems.

---

[52] https://bit.ly/2yrKLXJ

[53] https://bit.ly/2BC7wIG

These individuals don't need to be told how to solve problems. Let them work individually or collaboratively.

4. Make talent planning a key priority for your business. Examine not only who is working in your environment but also who should be. Who do you need to grow your business into new and emerging markets? Who do you need to create a collaborative and inclusive work environment? Include underrepresented and underutilized groups.
5. Social media is your friend. Start seeing LinkedIn, Facebook, Twitter, and other social media platforms as business resources rather than security threats and time wasters. Today's workforce learns not from being handed content but rather from utilizing connections.
6. Get diversity of thought. Make sure the right people are in the room, particularly those affected by the decision or closest to the work. This means going beyond the traditional group of people who are there. Really think about who could bring valuable input to the process.
7. Look for lattice opportunities for leadership development. With the flattening of organizations, the traditional steps of learning have gone away. Build skills through cross-functional assignments.

Inclusion is the solution to retention in today's ever-changing workplace. Every time an employee walks out of your door and, potentially, through the door of a competitor, you lose. You lose human capital, you lose institutional knowledge, and you lose brainpower. If you're not thinking every day about how you can retain the talent you have—and aren't doing something to make it happen—you lose. And, there is a lot to lose in the volatile business environment of the twenty-first century.

Today, says Rossman, "high-potential talent is not just expecting BASF to be thinking about inclusion; they're demanding that we already are inclusive. If we as a company don't meet that need, we're creating a revolving door. That's a business risk that none of us is comfortable taking."

7 Inclusion Is the Solution to Creativity and Innovation

We live in a time of mass disruption, with changes in technology, seismic demographic shifts, globalization and more. Disruption is a way of life. Disruption *requires* that we understand and leverage our differences to allow us to adapt and make constant, rapid changes in ever-shifting markets. We are further disrupted by the speed of change at work, in our communities, and in our educational settings. What happens globally impacts us daily.

As we move through this world of disruption with all of its complexities, we need a new approach to solve problems and create innovative solutions. We need a shift in thinking. We need a new way of having dialogue across differences so that we can address situations and problems as they emerge. We need a way to capitalize on the intelligence of differences—a way to take advantage of the opportunities that are continually coming our way.

The solution? Inclusion.

Inclusion is about getting everyone's voice heard to drive outcomes. It's about ensuring that everyone's perspective, experience, and talents are used to drive to a desired result.

Research by Abraham Carmeli, with Tel Aviv University in Israel, and Jane E. Dutton and Ashley E. Hardin with the Ross School of Business in Ann Arbor, Michigan, published by SAGE[54], found that "respectful engagement is indirectly related, through relationship information processing, to creative behavior at both the individual and team levels." They focused specifically on the impact of "respectful engagement" on creativity at both the individual and team levels. They conclude: "This series of studies has expanded the repertoire of theoretical lenses for examining how relationships at work matter for creativity, beyond networks of social exchange, by defining and testing how two core concepts—RE (respectful engagement) and RIP (relational information processing)—open up new levels of understanding about the relational roots of new ideas in work organizations."

---

[54] https://bit.ly/2ynQwGa

The ability of organizations to engage employees leads to creativity and innovation, both of which drive directly to the bottom line. It's worth the effort, as this research suggests, to use inclusion behaviors to drive belonging and engagement. That's exactly what Michelin is doing, and they're doing it well.

At Michelin, says Johnson, "we know that diverse teams are a major driver of innovation. In order for us to be leading edge in innovation, we've got to have perspectives from other cultures and from other countries to understand what our consumers are going to need today and in the future."

Not all leadership teams reflect the diversity that they espouse to support. Michelin's does. "After our re-organization in January 2018, our new leadership team radically changed," says Johnson. "For the first time ever, we have an African-American, a Hispanic-American, and three women, and the age demographic has dropped significantly—the oldest person on our leadership team is mid-50s. That is a huge step for us as an organization, and it's really quite exciting—even for a Baby Boomer, like myself, who is near the end of his career."

"One of the things that I have found fascinating is the fact that diverse teams are more successful, even though they don't always think that they are," says BASF's Rossman. "Diverse teams can feel like they struggle right up to the point where they have a really significant breakthrough. Homogeneous teams can feel like they're on the inside track—'our meetings are smooth and quick, and we'll solve the problem by lunch', they feel that they are going to find the best outcome right up to the moment when they don't, when they're not bringing in diverse perspectives. Homogeneous teams can be easier to manage because, right from the start, there's a sense of mutual agreement." But, when there's too much agreement, there is often not enough questioning and not enough innovation. Diverse teams may struggle a little more and ask tough questions that can be uncomfortable, says Rossman. "But in the end, wide-ranging industry studies demonstrate that when managed well, they come up with better solutions."

The realization of the impact of diversity and inclusion on creativity and innovation has not been lost on GM. "I think it's important and critical for any organization, but here, especially, at GM; employees need to be able to bring ideas forward and to actually spawn that creativity to tackle the challenges we face in a competitive industry," says Barrett. "It's about us being able to seek that technological edge—being able to be the game changer. We do that through diversity of thought, multiple perspectives, and an inclusive workforce."

Michelin is not alone in its recognition of the value that inclusion brings in terms of creativity and innovation. Mortenson's Weiss says: "We see inclusion as part of the evolution of our company —it's not a program or this year's training push. This is part of who we are as a company." Mortenson started its inclusion journey back in 2015, says Weiss, "When we recognized that we had a real desire to drive innovation at our company. We really believe that inclusion ties to innovation because you're bringing so many different perspectives to the table." The construction industry hadn't typically been one known for innovation, Weiss says. "We recognized that our industry was shifting, but we wanted to shift it even more. We saw that other industries had made a lot more progress in innovation, and we believed we could help move the construction industry along the journey as well."

Disruptive Innovation

Disruptive innovation is a concept created by Clayton M. Christensen, a Harvard Business School professor.[55] Many new developments started as disruptive innovation, which implies turning an expensive and complicated product into one that is simpler, less expensive and more accessible. The new product initially reaches new markets and goes to clients who are looking for low cost, may not be as demanding, and are willing to try products that are not yet perfect or mature. In many cases, the products steadily improve to meet the demanding needs of more sophisticated clients.

Everyday examples of this can be found in both technology (transitioning from a mainframe computer to a mini, to a desktop, to a laptop, and to a smartphone) and personal products (Crest's Whitestrips, which have eliminated a dentist visit by providing the same results at home). Looking to the future, we will see a disruptor/innovator with 3D printer technology (which

---

[55] https://bit.ly/1HT2VUc

may make some retail businesses and product manufacturers obsolete).

An important component of disruption is collaboration, because by joining the knowledge and innovation of different players, you will not only initiate disruptive products but also expedite their maturity. Collaboration, teamwork, and even working with competitors have all become standard practices and key elements of what makes a company competitive.

While many business leaders might not immediately connect the concepts of inclusion, creativity, and innovation, the reality is that inclusion and diversity are important elements in developing a creative and innovative culture. Businesses today operate in a climate of disruption driven by a global economy and technology. Responding effectively—and quickly—to disruptive forces is a must do, but it's not easy to do. It requires establishing a culture that is open to the input and voices of a wide diversity of people, both internal and external to the organization. We can't innovate if we don't have a wide range of inputs that are relevant to the markets we're attempting to influence.

Creativity involves the ability to pull together insights and input from a wide range of sources to drive breakthrough thinking. Innovation involves constantly finding new ways to attack problems and looking beyond traditional ways of producing and marketing products and services. Hiring a diverse workforce and then including the perspectives of all members of that diverse workforce are natural and proven ways to yield creative and innovative ideas.

After all, diversity doesn't just mean having a sprinkling of employees from a variety of racial or ethnic groups in your organization. Diversity means hiring people from a variety of age, socioeconomic, geographic, religious, educational, and experiential backgrounds as well as maintaining diversity in terms of racial, ethnic, and gender groups, because it makes sense for the business. While maintaining diversity is certainly an important element in creating an inclusive workplace, diversity alone is not enough.

Inclusion goes beyond simply having a diverse pool of employees. It's about engaging those employees so they become active contributors in the organization, coming up with great ideas and participating in decision-making. If you put a group of people with similar backgrounds in a room together and ask them to solve a problem, they're likely to come up with very similar ideas—and they're even more likely to agree with each other. This is because groupthink doesn't generally lead to innovative ideas.

But get a group of people from different backgrounds together, and they're likely to look at problems and opportunities in very different ways, magnifying the creativity of the entire group. That can be a great thing!

Challenging accepted patterns of thinking is an important element of innovation. If people in your organization tend to make comments like "well, that's the way we've always done it here," chances are there's not a lot of outside-the-box thinking going on. On the other hand, creating an inclusive environment and welcoming opposing points of view and challenges to the status quo allow organizations, the business community, and society in general to benefit.

Employees will be able to tap into diverse backgrounds, drawing upon a variety of personal, professional, and educational experiences that will lend to brainstorming fresh ideas and new ways of looking at things.

Ultimately, innovation is a product of an organization's human capital. If an organization is composed of a homogeneous labor pool with similar backgrounds and experiences, the organization can expect uniform thought processes and solutions. To generate new and different ideas, companies must be proactive and intentional about including as many diverse viewpoints as possible.

In the Harvard Business Review article "Teams Solve Problems Faster When They're More Cognitively Diverse,"[56] Alison Reynolds and David Lewis share the results of their research on Peter Robertson's AEM cube, which assesses the differences in how people approach change. Using a strategic executive exercise, they assessed the effectiveness of various groups based on their levels of cognitive diversity.

---

[56] https://bit.ly/2nAiRTF

The research is fascinating. As the chart below illustrates, and the study authors explain, "the three teams that completed the challenge in a good time (teams A, B, and C) all had diversity of both knowledge processes and perspective, as indicated by a larger standard deviation. The three that took longer or failed to complete (D, E, and F) all had less diversity, as indicated by a lower standard deviation."

Higher Cognitive Diversity Correlates with Better Performance

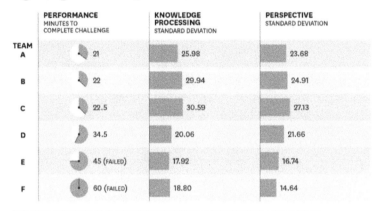

TEAM	PERFORMANCE MINUTES TO COMPLETE CHALLENGE	KNOWLEDGE PROCESSING STANDARD DEVIATION	PERSPECTIVE STANDARD DEVIATION
A	21	25.98	23.68
B	22	29.94	24.91
C	22.5	30.59	27.13
D	34.5	20.06	21.66
E	45 (FAILED)	17.92	16.74
F	60 (FAILED)	18.80	14.64

NOTE: COGNITIVE DIVERSITY IS CALCULATED AS STANDARD DEVIATIONS IN THINKING STYLES PRESENT ON EACH TEAM. SOURCE: ALISON REYNOLDS AND DAVID LEWIS USING THE AEM CUBE, A TOOL THAT ASSESSES DIFFERENCES IN THE WAY THAT PEOPLE APPROACH NOVEL SITUATIONS © HBR.ORG

They make an important point that should be a note of caution for business leaders and managers as they seek to engage employees: "If you look for it, cognitive diversity is all around— but people like to fit in, so they are cautious about sticking their necks out." Or, in the past, there may have been consequences for not agreeing with the way things have always been done, or for disagreeing with a particular leader whom everyone yields to.

There's additional research that illustrates quite compellingly the value of diverse teams. Here, researchers from MIT Sloan Management Review found that homogeneous teams came up with the wrong answer 30 percent of the time; that percentage dropped to 20 percent just by adding diversity to the team. Evan Apfelbaum (MIT Sloan Professor) said, "Diversity in the workplace can increase conflict. But research also suggests that if teams lack diversity, they will be more susceptible to making flawed decisions."

Writing for Scientific American in an article titled "How Diversity Makes Us Smarter,"[57] Katherine W. Phillips notes: "The key to understanding the positive influence of diversity is the concept of informational diversity. When people are brought together to solve problems in groups, they bring different information, opinions, and perspectives." This is really the crux of the argument, and it's a logical one. Her perspectives are amplified in a Harvard Business Review article titled "Why Diverse Teams are Smarter,"[58] written by David Rock and Heidi Grant. They write: "Diverse teams are more likely to constantly reexamine facts and remain objective. They may also encourage greater scrutiny of each member's actions, keeping their joint cognitive resources sharp and vigilant. By breaking up workplace homogeneity, you can allow your employees to become more aware of their own potential biases—entrenched ways of thinking that can otherwise blind them to key information and even lead them to make errors in decision-making processes."

The best innovator in the world today seems to be Apple. Apple revolutionized computing (Macintosh), digital media (Pixar), tablets (iPad), how we listen to music (iPod and iTunes), and turned our phones into total mobile devices (iPhone), to name just a few accomplishments. At every step of the way, Steve Jobs knew that competitors would soon be at his heels. Think about the tablet explosion that has occurred as a result of the iPad's popularity. Think about the explosion of Android phones that came after the iPhone launched.

Even Apple, in today's fast-changing and increasingly global environment, needs to constantly innovate. You can't rest on your laurels and hope to thrive off one great innovation. You can't afford to sit back and keep doing what has always worked in the past, because your competitors will copy you; they will improve on what has worked for you, and they will come up with new ways to do business that will make your current practices obsolete.

How do organizations keep up with the ongoing cycle of competition? Where does this much innovation come from? As

---

[57] https://bit.ly/1TY351h

[58] https://bit.ly/2e8tqvX

the Center for American Progress has pointed out, "Most people believe that innovation requires smarter people, better ideas. That premise, though intuitive, omits what may be the most powerful but least understood force for innovation: diversity."

Diversity of people and diversity of thought can remain untapped without a culture of inclusion. Creating that culture is critical for those who wish to harvest innovative ideas.

While numerous arguments can be made in support of inclusion as a driver of innovation, they all boil down to two factors. First, inclusion brings in a variety of inputs that help identify ongoing, unmet needs that require innovative solutions. Second, inclusion brings in a variety of viewpoints shaped by diverse past experiences, cultural backgrounds, individual knowledge, and unique thought processes that lay the broadest base for potential ideas.

It seems like a no-brainer. As America becomes more diverse, customers become more diverse. Similarly, an increasingly global marketplace greatly expands the realm of possible customers and the realm of differences among those customers.

Identifying with customers, then, means you identify not only with blue-collar Caucasian families in Indiana but also with first- or second-generation Hispanic families in Texas as well as young, tech-savvy Chinese college students in Beijing.

Wouldn't it be much easier to identify with diverse groups if you had members of those groups working for you? Why ask your North American employees to guess what new products or services the South Americans are interested in when you can just go down the hall and talk to your South American employees?

Clearly, identifying unmet or unarticulated needs is only half the innovation battle. Indeed, many of the most pressing issues facing organizations are already well known, like how do we reduce costs in the production process? How do we increase product usability? How do we add value to customers without drastically changing our service model?

Companies that can consistently answer these questions and meet the needs and wants of their customers will be in great shape to compete effectively, even in the most dynamic markets. And just as inclusion is the solution to identifying where innovation is needed, inclusion is the solution for driving continuous, effective innovation.

Innovation on the Edge

As Yann Cramer of Innovation Excellence points out in his article "Diversity Is a Source of Creativity and Resilience," innovation rarely happens at the core of any discipline, whether it's technology, business, music, or any other realm. It usually isn't the traditionalists at the heart of their field who find groundbreaking new ways of doing things. Instead, innovation happens at the edges of a discipline, where traditional viewpoints are challenged or complemented with knowledge from other areas of study.[59]

At Mortenson, says Weiss, "we have really had an uptick in enthusiasm around innovation and really understand that part of innovation means that you are welcoming all voices to the table." Being open to new ideas, even—and particularly—out-of-the-box ideas, really drives innovation and breakthrough ideas. "We're seeing some real energy here," Weiss says.

A Multitude of Lenses

When I am faced with a problem, I have a unique way of attempting to solve it based on my past experiences, my educational background, and the cultural influences that shape how I look at the world. This is the lens through which I see the world, so this is the lens through which I approach problem solving. You have your own lens, as does every employee in your company. These multiple lenses reflect a great value to your organization (pun intended). The more lenses through which your company can view a problem, the more likely you are to find a unique, innovative solution.

On the other hand, if your employees have nearly identical educational, cultural, and demographic backgrounds, you're likely to find that their perspectives are very similar as well, offering you access to fewer lenses. This is precisely why diversity is so important for innovation. If you have a multitude of lenses through which to view your world, you're going to have a multitude of ideas about how the world should and will

---

[59] https://bit.ly/2NvRFkc

look in the future and how to position your organization to be competitive in that future.

Embrace Your Diversity—Through Inclusion

Here's a key point and a misstep that far too many organizations make. While many companies are actively engaged in seeking out diverse employees, once these employees are hired, they are often expected to set aside their individuality and focus on a team identity. They're expected to go along with the flow, or the status quo, and they frequently face pressure to toe the company line, fit in with the culture, and otherwise assimilate. It's a pervasive process of taking richly diverse talent and perspectives and then diminishing the value of those perspectives by rewarding sameness of thought.

This is a mistake.

Keep in mind that while there is new research out about the diversity of thought already in organizations and its importance, let's not forget to harvest what comes from the diverse talent you're bringing into the organization. I recently sat in an executive session where a leader had an "aha moment" that while diverse talent had been hired, that same talent hadn't actually been tapped for innovation or been included! Let's not lose sight of the difference between diversity of individuals and diversity of thought. Let's not skip over racial, ethnic or gender diversity to diversity of thought simply because it's easier.

A recent study from Deloitte titled "The Radical Transformation of Diversity and Inclusion: The Millennial Influence" indicates that Millennials crave a collaborative environment where participation is encouraged, especially from those with different ideas and perspectives.[60] In fact, new thinking around diversity —driven to a large degree by the Millennial population— suggests that cognitive diversity, or differences in thoughts and problem-solving processes, is a key driver for innovation.

Writing for Inc., Keith Daly, Chief Claims Officer for Farmers Insurance, references the study and the concept of cognitive diversity and says: "Diversity of all kinds is extremely important, and so at Farmers we embrace a diversity of perspectives. We

---

[60] https://bit.ly/2IMfewM

believe inclusion draws on a rich variety of approaches and experiences and can lead to better decisions, a better organization, and a superior brand."[61]

Rather than seeking to avoid or minimize differences of opinion to get everyone on the same page, companies should instead be seeking to root out diverse opinions and areas of disagreement and dissension to drive innovation!

Inclusion Eclipses Ability

The Center for American Progress makes a strong argument for the value of inclusion within a diverse group of individuals relative to simply putting a group of smart people together.[62] As discussed earlier, diverse people have diverse lenses through which they see the world and look at problems. When allowed to complement one another, these lenses can create entirely new heuristics, or common methods of addressing problems, whereas a homogeneous group of very smart people will simply be better at using the lens they all started with.

Consider this analogy. If Person A sees the world through a blue lens and Person B sees the world through a yellow lens, having them collaborate allows you to look at a problem in blue, yellow, and green (i.e., blue mixed with yellow). However, if you have two of Person A, you simply have a deeper blue.

In other words, ten Albert Einsteins probably aren't as good at solving problems and innovating as a team of one Albert Einstein, one Shirley Engelmeier, and eight employees at eight different organizations in eight different countries around the world!

Communicate to Innovate

Having a diverse range of viewpoints and insights is crucial for innovation, and your ability to utilize those diverse viewpoints increases exponentially when you have robust communication. If you have ten diverse individuals working separately on a project, you benefit from ten different viewpoints. When you include all

---

[61] https://bit.ly/2OariFX

[62] https://ampr.gs/1ub2KGf

these people in one discussion, you benefit from a sharing of ideas in which one group member can use his or her unique perspective to build off an undeveloped thought from another group member. Likewise, a wide array of experiences and knowledge can help the group think critically and avoid groupthink - the tendency for a group of like-minded people to be so concerned about maintaining harmony that they overlook creative alternatives.

It's an approach that seems to be a no-brainer; it's simply common sense. But it's also an approach backed up by research. In their report "Respect as an engine for new ideas: Linking respectful engagement, relational information processing and creativity among employees and teams," researchers from Tel Aviv University in Israel and the Ross School of Business in Ann Arbor, Michigan, share the findings from four studies.[63]

The researchers point out that "in particular, if individuals interrelate in ways that foster respect, relationships serve as means for endogenously resourcing individuals and fostering creativity."

The reverse, of course, is also true. In environments where employees are *not* treated respectfully, where their input and insights are not treated with respect, where risk-taking is neither supported nor encouraged, and where diverse input is not sought, creativity and innovation will not flourish.

In an increasingly competitive business environment, diverse inputs are a must have. Companies that however inadvertently shut off these inputs do so at their own risk.

And the Innovators?

Everyone can innovate: every gender, every age group, every ethnicity. All can be brilliant. All can be creative. But if I must tip my hat to the real rock stars of innovation in the workforce of tomorrow, it's going to be the newly emerging cohorts, Generation Y, and, right behind them, Generation Z.

Why? Because they haven't yet been beaten down by the system (although Generation Y may be losing some of their original zeal

---

[63] https://bit.ly/2NupUZr

as the organizations they work for tamp down their natural inclination toward input and innovation).

- "We tried that before, and it didn't work."
- "You don't understand how things are done around here."
- "Until you've worked in the industry for X years, you really don't get it."

These are the kinds of statements and sentiments that squash innovation.

The same impact, of course, can occur on the other edge of the age spectrum.

- "You're not a digital native; what can you possibly know about...?"
- "Why do you keep beating a dead horse?"
- "You're not in touch with the younger generations..."

Innovators come in all shapes, sizes, demographics, and geographies. Yes, the newer entrants to the workforce who *are* digital natives have much to bring, and their voices should be listened to. But, so should the voices of their more senior cohorts.

The business world of the future will belong to Gen Y and Gen Z, and companies looking to succeed in that new world absolutely must include them in planning for it. The speed with which the global economy and business world are changing cannot be overstated. Today's competitive landscape is increasingly influenced by decision-makers and markets from around the globe, and, as time goes by, this globalization will only continue to spread. Gen Y and Gen Z represent the best weapon available to many organizations as they transition into an increasingly global environment, so it is critical that organizations learn how to get the most from this new generation. And the importance of knowledge workers to an organization has grown steadily in recent years and shows no signs of slowing.

And if your company is hoping to attract a share of the retiring Baby Boomer market to benefit from their massive amounts of disposable income and interest in living life to the fullest, you'll need to understand that group.

Marketing to Latinas? Marketing to African-Americans? Marketing to young, white men? Hopefully you get the point. It's not about diversity for diversity's sake. It's about *strategic* diversity—and, then, creating a culture of inclusion to gain the benefit of the diversity.

Ultimately, inclusion is key to innovation because inclusion increases the collective brain of an organization, adding new ideas and allowing those ideas to interact, combine, and improve. Diverse ideas are key to this process, and business leaders need to remember that innovation doesn't happen in the comfort zone of any discipline. It happens at the fringes, where diverse viewpoints challenge the status quo and provide new solutions to old problems.

But diversity alone is not enough. It's just the starting point. You can hire the most diverse workforce imaginable, but to be truly innovative, you must be collaborative and inclusive. It's not enough to simply have diversity among your employees—you must capitalize on that diversity through inclusion. Problem-solving techniques and problem solvers themselves build off one another. Indeed, they thrive off one another. Bringing in people with a wide array of experiences, skills, insights, and thought processes creates a rich environment for creativity and innovation, but only if you seek their perspectives and actually listen to them!

The whole is greater than the sum of its parts, and a diverse group of creative thinkers will outperform a homogeneous group of similar-minded geniuses. The key is to be diverse, to be inclusive, and to foster effective communication.

In the modern global economy, companies can't afford to stand still and rest on their history of what worked. What may once have been a game-changing business strategy or novel invention can be copied or made obsolete in an instant by competitors from any corner of the globe. To maintain a competitive advantage and continue to be profitable, businesses need to be able to innovate.

So, what does innovation actually mean? The term suggests cutting-edge technological advancements and futuristic inventions. However, innovation is much more than the process of scientific invention. While these types of breakthroughs certainly represent the possible end results of innovation, a complete definition also includes creativity, insight, and challenging traditional ways of thinking and operating. In other words, innovation is both the idea and the outcome. It's not enough to simply think of new ideas; companies must generate some profitable use to benefit from them.

Why is innovation so critical for modern companies? It's no secret that we live and work in an increasingly global economy. As your business is exposed to more and more markets, you will need to constantly find new ways to cater to the changing and diverse needs of those markets and to compete with businesses that may already be capitalizing on the innovation. One way to do this is to find innovative, new ways to meet the needs of a variety of cultures and tastes—this is exactly what companies like Coca-Cola, McDonald's, Nabisco and others do as they tap into new, and increasingly diverse, markets. Their subtle, market-specific variations on products are great examples of how these companies have been innovative as they've attempted to expand the reach of their products to a global environment.

Certainly, innovation can lead to significant competitive advantage that creates something different or better than what the competition has to offer. Competitive advantage allows companies to outperform others in terms of market share, cost savings, and revenue generation. An innovative new production technique, for example, can allow a company to produce its products more cost effectively than its major competitors, helping it send more of its revenue to the bottom line. But competitive advantages do not last forever.

The Ford Model T was a great thing in its time. So were VHS tapes and newspapers. But the world continues to change around us, and we need to change with it. Companies that create a culture of innovation and consistently capitalize on new ideas and ways of thinking can stay ahead of the competition and ahead of changing needs among the markets they serve.

Let's consider some of the recent major impacts on companies that failed to innovate quickly enough to address emerging markets and the massive impacts of new technology.

If you were a taxi driver, or taxi company, in San Francisco before 2009, you likely had a pretty good thing going: lots of tourists, lots of nightlife, lots of reasons to flag a taxi to go from one place to another. Then something happened: innovation. Disruptive innovation in the form of Uber, a ridesharing company that has taken the world—and the transportation industry—by storm. Uber and Lyft—another ridesharing service —have upended the taxi industry, not only in San Francisco but also around the world! It's highly likely that most taxi services never saw it coming!

The same could likely be said about the plethora of big-brand, brick-and-mortar retail stores that dominated the consumer market for decades. But then the Internet—and, specifically, Amazon—emerged. It's being called the retail apocalypse, and stalwart retail companies like Sears, Payless, Toys "R" Us, Macy's, and a myriad of others are feeling the pinch.

Through a review of publicly available information, 24/7 Wall Street did an analysis of the retail landscape, including store closings, bankruptcies, and liquidations, to identify those closing the most stores. As reported in USA Today, they are:

- Toys "R" Us – 735 store closings
- Rite Aid – 600 store closings
- Subway – 500 store closings
- Teavana – 379 store closings
- The Children's Place – 300 store closings[64]

Retail Dive, which is maintaining a running list of retail bankruptcies, reported in May 2018 the following bankruptcies that had been filed just in the first few months of the year:

- January 9 – A'gaci
- January 11 – Kiko USA
- February 4 – Bon-Ton
- March 6 – The Walking Company
- March 19 – Claire's
- April 6 – Nine West
- May 14 – Rockport[65]

---

[64] https://bit.ly/2Cv4lal

[65] https://bit.ly/2neEZnv

With these companies and many others, numerous impacts ultimately mark their demise. But other companies that are renowned for capturing the hearts and minds of their employees and cultivating their ideas seem to thrive even in a turbulent economy marked by disruptive technologies and increasing competition. They thrive because they do things differently. They stimulate change. They remain attuned to what people are thinking—not just their employees but also their markets. And they adjust their practices, and sometimes even their products, to address these changing needs.

They recognize that the sum of the parts can be greater than the whole.

The innovative companies get it. Think Apple. Think Netflix. Think Square. Think Tencent. They top the list of Fast Company's most innovative companies in 2018.[66] A decade ago, many of the companies on Fast Company's list didn't even exist. There are also, though, some companies on the list that represent the old guard—The Washington Post, Ford Foundation and Gucci. What separates these companies from those like Blockbuster, RadioShack, Kodak and a wide range of others that have failed?

The ability to innovate and/or the willingness to listen to their employees' ideas.

If an employee came to you in 1975 and told you he'd invented the digital camera, what would you do? If you were Kodak, you shoved him into a closet and hoped the product never reached the mass market. That's exactly what happened with Steven Sasson at Kodak. His bosses were unimpressed. "They were convinced that no one would ever want to look at their pictures on a television set," Sasson told The New York Times.[67]

So, we come back to the ability to innovate and/or the willingness to listen to employees' ideas. As we pointed out earlier, our Global Inclusion Index showed that companies that used more inclusion behaviors created a culture where 25 percent of employees were more motivated by their jobs and 12

---

[66] https://bit.ly/2Hxrubi

[67] https://nyti.ms/2l3ZdwA

percent were more willing to share ideas and think of ways to improve the workplace.

The companies that are succeeding today and that will succeed in the future will be fueled by the kind of innovation that comes from remaining aware of and responding to the myriad changes that impact companies every day. That means recognizing that it's not just the people at the top of the organization who have all the great ideas. It means valuing the input and perspective of each and every member of the organization—recognizing that you never know where that next great insight or idea may come from. It means seeking out diverse opinions to make sure your organization isn't just responding to one narrow niche in the market but is prepared to hear and address multiple perspectives from multiple sources.

Take action. Resolve not to miss any good ideas. Embrace innovation by embracing the voices of your employees and customers—all their voices. Remember: Inclusion is a business strategy that drives innovation.

8 It's About Selling More Goods and Services

It should be no secret to anyone reading this book that we are living in an increasingly global, interconnected, and diverse world. In the early twentieth century, an American producer or service provider could get along just fine focusing on the American market or even a regional or state market. Even if a company wanted to enter a foreign market, the logistical challenges would have dissuaded all but the most ambitious. Similarly, domestic organizations had little to fear from competitors abroad, but those days are long gone.

Today, not only is it what you're selling, but also *how* you're selling it. In our recent work with a large retail client executive, the client referred to the massive changes affecting retailers due to online shopping as "the retail apocalypse." The Internet has had a massive impact on how goods and services are sold—locally, domestically, and abroad. Emerging technologies—like artificial intelligence, machine learning, blockchain, etc.—are likely to only add to the rapidly shifting marketplace. The ability for machines to learn based on the interactions they have, or repeated attempts to do something, promises to upend the workplace as machines can increasingly take on the tasks currently performed by human beings. IBM's Watson is probably the best example.

In order to address these shifts, as we've emphasized throughout this book, we *need* diversity and we *need* inclusion—not to check a box, but to drive business!

Big Business Benefits From I&D

Inclusion and diversity are business imperatives. Companies that have ethnic and gender diversity outperform their peers in terms of being more likely to capture new markets and get new revenue. In fact, consumer research points to evidence that black, Hispanic and Asian consumers can serve as cultural multipliers or culture influencers.

GM is another company that really understands this. "We look at how being able to bring a diverse array of talent into the company and making sure we have a culture of inclusion to empower them brings ideas forward to ultimately impact the market," says Barrett. And it's not just in subjective ways. "We look at many different dynamic dimensions, whether it's our ethnic share of brand, which is how our products are winning in the marketplace with African-American buyers, Hispanic buyers, Asian-American buyers, women, etc.," he says. "Being able to have a laser focus on each of these constituencies and being able to not just compete but to win in the marketplace is absolutely critical."

What Rules?

When I wrote this section the first time, in 2012, it was called "New Rules, New Game." But today, with the level of disruption and adaptation needed by businesses hoping to sell more and be more profitable, it seems that there isn't even time to create rules or even rename the game. In 2012:

- If you wanted a ride, you called a limo or cab company. Now, you simply ask Uber or Lyft.
- If you wanted to buy groceries, you went to the grocery store and filled your cart as you walked aisle to aisle among the shelves—now you fill your cart online and the groceries are delivered directly to your door.
- If you wanted to make an appointment, get restaurant reservations, or complete a wide range of other transactions, you called a business directly. Today, Alexa can do that for you.
- If you needed to see a doctor, you made an appointment and went to your local clinic. Today you can go online to see a doctor who's not even located in your city, state, or country.

These massive shifts impacting industries require new ways of thinking and, in many cases, new forms of partnerships. The healthcare industry, for instance, is seeing rampant merger and acquisition activity as partnerships form between traditional players and technology giants—like Google, Amazon, and Apple.

As Tim Cook of Apple has illustrated through both words and deeds[68], the ability to stay relevant and reach new markets will require cultural savvy driven through strategic partnerships. In

---

[68] https://bit.ly/2PoYJkK

early 2018, for instance, Cook announced a partnership with Malala Fund to provide financial support that will allow the fund to double the number of grants provided in India and Latin America. There's the way to stay both connected and relevant.

To be agile, a company needs to have an innovative culture. It needs to be able to come up with creative, new ways to make transitions and efficiently convert resources from one use to another. Inclusive cultures utilize their diverse knowledge, backgrounds, and thought processes to create an environment that thinks outside the box and breeds creativity.

Out of the Ivory Tower

Years ago, American companies like McDonald's created products catered to American appetites, and the rest of the world literally ate them up. Hollywood movies, created for American audiences and based on American culture, were in high demand around the globe. While there is certainly still a demand for American culture and American products, developing countries now want to consume goods and services that reflect their own local tastes. And the increased ability of domestic companies to give them just that means America's monopoly on consumers is a thing of the past. The emergence of Bollywood is a prime example.

India, one of the world's fastest-growing economies and largest markets, has developed its own sophisticated entertainment industry. As nations around the world develop the capacity to meet the demands of their populations, foreign companies will have to cater to the unique needs of local groups.

Inclusion is key to satisfying these diverse markets. If you are a culturally homogeneous organization struggling to break into the Brazilian market, you shouldn't be surprised. How can you hope to compete with local firms or diverse, inclusive multinational firms if you don't understand the culture or the market you are trying to lure over to your products or services?

Companies that employ a variety of diverse individuals have a great advantage over those that don't, and this doesn't just mean middle management. You need sophisticated executives with a diversity of backgrounds to help you coordinate your global strategy, because every aspect of your business must be able to successfully navigate a range of cultures and tastes. For example, it's not just about figuring out what type of food people like in your target market. A hilarious commercial in one country might be extremely offensive in another. What is polite when dealing with one country's regulators might be aloof or rude to regulators in another nation.

We Get It...Sort Of

The changes I am seeing today in business that I talked about at the beginning of this book—changes related to technology, automation, globalization, and the economy—all require new conversations. Collectively, we need new and more varied voices at the table. Sameness of individuals and thoughts within organizations does not lead to innovation and business success. Sameness yields mediocrity and lack of imagination. Sameness leaves us disconnected from emerging markets and emerging ways of thinking. It leaves us in the dust. If we're not part of the new conversations and if we're not having these conversations with the broad array of constituencies that represent our markets, we will not survive in the new global business normal.

Businesses exist to serve markets by providing them with goods and services that they value. In a rapidly changing business environment that is increasingly competitive, increasingly global, and increasingly impacted by new advances in technology, organizations can't afford to ignore the voices of their markets or the voices of their employees. Inclusion is a business strategy!

9 Overcoming the Stuck State

Organizations around the country have been focusing on diversity and inclusion for a long time—for years, for decades. I know because I've been there beside them along the way. And yet, many organizations despite their best intentions, concerted efforts, and significant investments in people and programs are not achieving the results they desire. They may make some progress but, inevitably, see that progress stop, even backslide.

I call this the stuck state.

There are a number of reasons the stuck state has emerged to stymie the I&D efforts of organizations large and small.

STUCK STATE REASON #1 – The confusion between inclusion and diversity

One reason the stuck state has occurred is that there is a huge disconnect on what the words inclusion and diversity mean. Some executives I interview think they're the same. Some think inclusion is a more politically correct term for diversity. The bottom line is that I see the term inclusion used interchangeably with diversity. Let me emphasize what I hope by now is obvious: these terms are not interchangeable!

While this is a very basic concept, let's revisit the definitions of inclusion and diversity; they are also provided in detail in the Introduction.

Diversity—noun—describes the differences between people.

Now, let's contrast that with inclusion.

Inclusion—to include - verb: a call to action—includes everyone's voice and talents. You have to *do something* to include someone.

The critical part of this definition is that you need to *do* something to include people. You must demonstrate inclusion behaviors and inclusive leader competencies to create a culture of inclusion.

From a diversity perspective, a lot of this work is done in talent acquisition and talent management. It is about readying diverse talent, talent based on primary dimensions like race, gender, and ethnicity. This is hard work!

A lot of work has been done on recruiting diverse talent. Little work has been done on creating a culture of inclusion. I always find it interesting that the two aren't connected in organizations. Talent acquisition is responsible for getting the talent in the door with no regard for how long they'll stay or whether they are successful long term. Who is responsible for that?

The acquisition of talent is very different from the inclusion of diverse talent. I was a speaker at a talent conference recently. Nearly every leader there was responsible for bringing diverse talent into the organization. When asked, not one of them was working to create a culture of inclusion that would ensure the same talent stayed! How can this be?

Because of unease with the topic, we parcel it out into different little chunks of responsibility. It's really time to change that!

STUCK STATE REASON #2 – We speak different languages

In our last six client engagements, we have had the privilege of working with the executive teams, including the CEOs, of Fortune 500 companies. I consider this an honor and a privilege. I also understand that the reason we get this privilege is that we are business-centric. We take a business-centric approach to help companies drive better business results. We are, first and foremost, *business people.* We use business principles to help businesses sell more goods and services amid a shifting environment—internal and external—of inclusion and diversity.

My corporate experience was on the business side of the house; I was responsible for sales primarily in consumer product goods (CPG) companies—specifically Brown & Williamson and Frito-Lay. I have never been in HR, but, from my first days in a corporate environment, I saw how creating a culture of inclusion could drive business results. I saw whose voices counted—and I saw whose were excluded.

Recently we were having a conversation with a potential client. We were speaking to the HR team who ran the programs related to "Inclusive Leader Executive Development." Now, I have great respect for the HR business partners who work with businesses to drive business results. However, we often speak very different languages. For example, as we were explaining our work, one of the HR people on the call asked: "How does this align to cross-cultural and intercultural bodies of work?" My response: "It doesn't. What we work with are globally validated inclusion behaviors that drive to results." Those results? Selling more goods and services more cost-effectively!

That's the language of business, and that's the language that business executives—members of the C-suite—respond to.

The language and the conversation that this HR representative was using has zero appeal to the executives of the organizations we work with. I've found that in-group speak (like "cross-cultural and intercultural bodies of work") makes executives feel excluded and uncomfortable. They're responsible for growth, revenue, talent, and a huge list of business priorities too numerous to mention.

Inclusion and diversity initiatives should have a clear tie and connection with HR, says Michelin's Johnson. "That's where I think we have made a lot of progress," he says. Johnson's predecessor was not part of HR, he says; but he welcomed the opportunity for the D&I team be a part of HR because, he says, "our HR colleagues and, in particular, our career management team represent an opportunity to contribute to the high performance, or what we at Michelin call the boost potential list." At Michelin, says Johnson, "we look at those 30–40 years old and, sometimes younger, to try to recognize and identify potential." The D&I team, he says, looks at high potential through a different lens from HR. Collaboration and teamwork between these groups, says Johnson, has led to "a much more diverse list of high-potential employees, and it's also prompted us to maybe be a little more willing to challenge the status quo—to move some people a little faster than we would have." It has, he says, "been fruitful for the entire organization."

If we, as people in the field, can't break the work we do down to something that supports the business, we are never going to get there. I do mean never. As you can see, this harkens back to our discussion of diversity fatigue earlier in the book.

The issue is pervasive and stems back even to college and post-graduate education programs. Recently, I guest lectured for the MBA program of a highly prestigious business school. I spent 90 minutes talking about inclusion as a driver for business. If anyone needs to firmly understand this concept, it's MBA students! But at the end of my lecture, a very learned professor asked me: "Does this really work for businesses?"

As with the HR professional, we were speaking two different languages. I was speaking the language of business—he was an expert in prejudice and stereotyping. I was speaking about real issues—important issues that certainly do impact business and the sales of goods and services. But, it's the translation of I&D in-group speak to I&D as a business strategy that will move the needle to more inclusive behaviors, more inclusive environments, and, ultimately, more sales of goods and services.

This may seem like subtle distinction to many, but it's an important one. It's a distinction that resonates with the C-suite. And because they're the ones who make decisions, they're the ones we need to resonate with. And we do.

STUCK STATE REASON #3 – We haven't treated it as a business issue

How is it that this one area of human capital has been reduced to tactics or activities? Let me give you an example of this. We were on the panel at the Conference Board in New York City. We had just launched InclusionINC's InclusionSCORECARD®. We spent 60 minutes explaining why we created a business-centric scorecard modeled after Harvard's Balanced Scorecard of the early 90s. We had explained using four quadrants what the strategic linkage to the business could be, how this type of approach was *critical* to the success of this work, and many other compelling business points.

At the end of that, the first question I got was "Just what's the one thing you could do to make a difference here?" Really? OK, this may be a rant, *and* I gave my same answer I usually give on this. "If I knew the answer to this, I'd own an island, and I'd invite you all there to visit." Then I posed these questions: "In what other area of business do you do just one thing to be successful? If you're launching a new product line or opening a new business location, you'd never do just one thing. For R&D of the latest innovation, there isn't one thing."

At Sodexo, says Harris, "one of the first things that was done in the U.S. was to develop a scorecard to have a focus on some culture change drivers on our journey." The scorecard, she says, "allows the company to drive accountability throughout the organization by linking D&I goals to performance and financial metrics." At Sodexo, leaders are incentivized to achieve goals— ten percent of their salaries are connected to measures of representation, the movement of diverse talent, and engagement activities to drive inclusion. "Payout takes place regularly— that's how serious Sodexo is taking it," she says.

STUCK STATE REASON #4 – Executives and leaders tend to avoid the word diversity

As we've worked with corporations around the country, over and over again we've seen an interesting sort of avoidance of the word diversity. It's a word that can generate sensitivity and concerns—particularly among white male populations who have often been left out of inclusion and diversity efforts or believe that inclusion and diversity isn't about them. And, after all, as we've already seen, the makeup of most senior leadership teams and corporate boards still tends to be very white male dominant.

We've seen this avoidance play out in a variety of ways. In some cases, before we begin our executive leadership and unconscious bias work, members of the C-suite will say: "Wait! Let's not take action yet. We need to look at our strategy again." Okay, but you did that two years ago. This work is the most potent form of action you can take—now!

This is not a Harvard Business Review-researched comment. This is a Shirley theory. Over and over I have seen mass avoidance behaviors from C-suites. The themes are many; I'll lift up just a few anecdotes to make my point here.

Executives are used to being very smart and knowing exactly what to do. They're used to being decision-makers. But when it comes to building an inclusive culture, they frequently *don't know* what to do. Avoidance is the path of least resistance. We've sat through many executive sessions where silence is the name of the game—people just don't contribute. These are leaders who are running massive organizations, and they have lots of opinions about many important business issues—except maybe this one.

In some cases, they're simply afraid to say anything. The #MeToo movement may have fueled some of their anxiety: "I don't know what I can and can't say."

Yet, while these senior leaders, many of them white males, may bristle at the term diversity, they need to learn to embrace the concept—not of diversity for diversity's sake, but through inclusion as a business imperative. Inclusion is for everyone— even white males.

STUCK STATE REASON #5 – We can't find qualified people

This belief is for real. While writing this book, I had an executive tell me they needed to make sure they had "qualified people." I hope my face didn't show what I was thinking. Basically, this executive was telling me that if he put women or people of color in positions, he was lowering his standards because they weren't as qualified as white men.

This was a business-to-consumer (B2C) company where most people could readily learn the skills and competencies of the business. This company wasn't looking for neurophysicists! They needed great managers and leaders. This conversation happened to occur the week that the first woman CEO—Stacey Cunningham—was named to the NYSE. It took 226 years for that to happen!

I am going to say something sacrilegious now. I think there was a time when women and people of color *didn't* have enough experience to lead, back in the 70s, 80s and 90s. It was NOT because we weren't smart enough; it was simply because we weren't given the same developmental opportunities as men.

However, in the year 2019, if an organization can't find "qualified" women and people of color, they don't know where to look or they don't have a culture of inclusion that knows what to do with differences.

It's something that most organizations will bump into at one time or another, but there are some things they can do to help get unstuck with this problem

Large organizations, like GM for instance, that are doing a good job of aligning action with strategy and measuring success have the ability to identify areas within their organizations that might be stuck, as well as areas that can serve as best practice examples. "Especially in a big organization like GM, there are a lot of places that are doing it right and seeing success," says Barrett. "So, how are you able to capture those lessons and then apply them to other areas where they're maybe not having the same levels of success? That's what we try to do, and to me, it is the definition of a culture of inclusion—being able to include all of the different things that you're doing and being able to share best practices across your company is critical."

One of the solutions that Walmart's Fan and others point to is the need for inclusion and diversity efforts to be not just one-off events, or programs, but to be cultural shifts that ensure every aspect of the organization's interactions with people—potential employees, employees, customers, business partners, and others —is inclusive. From a talent perspective, that's not something that occurs only during the hiring process. That's why Walmart uses a CDI (Culture Diversity Inclusion) scorecard to measure inclusion across multiple factors—not just representation, but also talent mobility from new hires, promotions, demotions, lateral moves, voluntary and involuntary terminations, and cultural perceptions of inclusion and belonging.

"If you don't change the environment, if you don't change the culture, you can bring people in, but they won't stay because the environment does not truly include them, grow them, and empower them to unleash their full potential and fulfill their career aspirations," Fan says.

STUCK STATE REASON #6 – Unwillingness to intentionally sponsor underrepresented talent

Here is the single most controversial thing that I'll say in this book. Why do we need to give extra advantage to women and people who are ethnically and racially different? Or Millennials whose insights are needed to capture the sales of the organizations' constituencies? Or? Or? Or?

White men have had an "in" when it comes to being positioned to move into roles of power across virtually all industries. Take a look at the board makeup of Fortune 500 companies, and you'll see a sea of older white men. Take a look around the C-suite at most organizations; you'll see the same thing. We've explored some of the reasons behind this. Sadly, the disparities begin at a very young age as those with connections, or privilege, move beyond those without.

Female representation in the workplace is one example. In a study published in Science[69], Lin Bian (psychologist at the University of Illinois) and Andrei Cimpian (Professor of Psychology at New York University) address the issue of women opting out of certain fields of study at a very early age. The research is shocking. According to Bian and Cimpian, as early as age 6, girls are identifying their male classmates as being smarter than they are.

This impacts the talent acquisition formula. By the time girls make their way from kindergarten to graduation, they have already dismissed any number of careers that might position them more competitively against the males they will compete with when they enter the workplace.

Walmart has a formal mentoring program, including sponsorship, as well as other efforts like lean-in circles for current and potential female managers (men also are able to participate). Sponsorship is different from mentorship, says Fan, "because, as sponsors, leaders are going to commit personal, organizational resources to selected associates or selected high-potential talent and speak on their behalf at the table when there are promotion decisions being made." Sponsorship, says Fan, generally results from mentor relationships. "You've got to know someone well before you would sponsor her or him. You can't have anyone coming up to you and say, 'Hey, can you be my sponsor?' if you don't already have a relationship established. So, let's start at the mentoring relationship; then after we see merit, quality and needed competency, we may develop and evolve the mentoring relationship into a sponsorship."

---

[62] https://bit.ly/2QEazYu

Sodexo also has a sponsorship practice as part of its talent development work, says Harris. "Leaders in D&I work with the market segment executive leadership teams to identify the diversity mix, the high-potentials, and how the company can ensure that these individuals are identified for opportunities."

"We have some leaders who have sponsored more than one individual," she says. "They provide them with guidance, direction, hands on experiences, and training." The key, though, is support—lifting these individuals up so that they are visible, have had the training and opportunities to help position them to move into new roles, and to ensure that they are not overlooked when opportunities emerge.

Intentional sponsorship can help by giving women—and other underrepresented groups—a hand up. The companies we spoke with have taken specific steps to provide employees—especially women and people of color—with opportunities that can help to position them for future leadership opportunities.

That is where intentional sponsorship can take you.

STUCK STATE REASON #7 – sending women and people of color to development programs will change the status quo

I had a conversation with a CEO at a client site about the concept of "managing your own career." I told him I love the idea once we get to the point where people could promote themselves and give themselves pay raises. While we both laughed, I really wasn't trying to be funny.

The most preposterous scenario I see in this work is sending women and people of color to programs to help them navigate the culture of their organizations. This rang true the most for me when I was sitting with a group of high potential women in a consumer products self-development conference. The title of the program was "How to Have Conversations with Difficult Leaders." In that moment I was quite sure that none of the women in the room were the people that the company really needed to have these conversations with! Where were their leaders? Where were the men?

The only way change can take place is when executives (who are still primarily white men) are in the room understanding why we need the change to a culture of inclusion.

Beyond the Stuck State: A Concerted Focus

When Michelin's Herb Johnson stepped into his role, he says, "We were experiencing what is commonly referred to as diversity fatigue." Michelin had been talking about diversity for more than fifteen years, he said, "but, quite frankly, people were either tired of hearing about diversity or felt like 'Okay, yeah, diversity, so what?'" Johnson was charged with bringing more visibility, awareness, and energy to the topic.

His first step was to benchmark what other organizations were doing. He found that most had moved beyond diversity to focus on inclusion. In 2015, that's the approach that he began to take with Michelin, and we're proud to have been part of that journey. Michelin was able to get beyond the stuck state. Their most recent recognition confirms their success.

Still, he is quick to point out that the company's work toward building a culture of inclusion has not always been easy— change never is. "Not everyone has embraced it at the same time, and it has taken a while for it to stick." Creating a culture of inclusion is, in truth, not a task that can be marked as done. It is an ongoing effort.

At GM, the focus is also on inclusion, says Barrett. "We all think diversity is the big picture, but inclusion is the test—do people really, in fact, have the ability to bring their ideas to the forefront? Are they empowered to do so? Are they listened to?"

It's not a quick process. It's a journey. Sometimes, says Harris with Sodexo, "It feels so awfully slow." But, she stresses, shifting to a culture of inclusion is "an incremental change." Forward movement should be the focus. "As long as you're making progress, as long as you keep it on the table as an area of focus tied to your company values and core business objectives, you'll keep your leaders engaged." And, eventually, you'll drive needed changes.

Never lose sight, Harris says, of what you're here to do—"We're here to ensure we are providing quality of life experiences for our employees and everyone we serve each day." At Sodexo, she says, and likely at any company, "there's no way you can do that without having a cross-section of perspectives that are informing what that looks like for the various groups we serve."

Keeping the mandate for inclusion part of a business conversation that is continually tied to the important things happening in your organization is the best way to avoid the stuck state, says Harris. "It's important to step back and recognize how we're evolving; let's not just make this about the data—this is us. This is our people; this is how we're serving the people we need to serve."

Walmart's Fan said if we don't take steps to change the environment and the culture, we can't expect to bring in new, diverse team members that we can retain. They simply won't stay if they don't feel that they're part of an inclusive environment where their voices are heard, and their perspectives are valued. This requires a concerted focus on inclusion, beyond diversity, that makes the real difference. "That's why we measure both spectrums—diversity and inclusion—on our scorecards," he says. "We look at it for different levels of our management pipelines—entry-, mid-, and senior-level and corporate officers." That data tells an important story—one version of truth, he says —and may point to specific areas where the stuck state is in full motion.

The flip side of the stuck state would be continual motion, continual improvement. In truth, being inclusive isn't an event or a milestone—it's a journey. Because the world is continually changing, and your markets—consumer and employee—are continually changing, it's a journey that never ends. But it's a journey that shouldn't stall, get stuck, or decline. It's a constant movement forward marked by measurement, course correction, and a continued focus on creating, nurturing, and maintaining a culture that includes everyone.

INCLUSION AS AN ACCELERATOR

10 Strategy and Accountability

When I ask clients what their strategy looks like, I frequently get answers about their representation on a dashboard. I think this is important. And yet, without the staying power of supporting the business, it won't matter. I then ask, "Why are you focused on a diverse workforce? Why do you want or need a culture of inclusion? How is that being linked to your overall business strategy?"

Early on, we understood that a business-centric strategy was needed. We understood that without linking inclusion to the business case, no one would care. That's why we launched the InclusionSCORECARD®. The framework **integrates** the work of both operational and talent leaders to drive **sustainable** culture change. InclusionINC customizes this approach to meet the needs of your organization and to achieve four key outcomes:

- Does your company have the right talent in place to drive business growth with existing and emerging customer or consumer segments?
- Does your corporate culture support inclusion at all levels of the organization and incorporate activities that support an inclusive workplace culture?
- Will your company translate inclusive behaviors into targeted performance objectives for managers and supervisors?
- Does your company have key external relationships to drive your strategy for emerging growth markets and to achieve business results?

Using the SCORECARD® we examine quantitative and qualitative data to provide a multigenerational plan of action. It's important to measure what is happening beyond the final metrics.

A key component of our work is measuring what happens behind the numbers. We propose measuring who is getting invited to leadership programs, who's included in special cross-functional projects, and who is mentored—to name just a few measures. The bottom line is if talent isn't prepared, it is now the problem of the leader. What a switch this is! The individual who is different—whether they are introverted, a Millennial, a woman, a person of color, or a non-engineer—requires the leader to provide them opportunities to move ahead organizationally.

We recommend that business people **own** career development.

While business leaders and their HR and I&D staff members are never done when it comes to creating a culture of inclusion and belonging, having specific goals, objectives, and metrics to monitor success is critical for ensuring accountability.

In fairness to most leaders, it has never been clearly defined for them what the accountability is. If it has been, it was easier to look at the composition of talent with primary diversity dimensions, primarily women and people of color.

We are suggesting putting rigor into what happens behind those metrics; again, who is getting tapped for high-visibility projects and who is being informally mentored? We are also clear that leaders need the skills and competencies—inclusive leader competencies and inclusion behaviors that can be observed and measured.

How Leaders in I&D Measure Their Progress

HR, D&I, and talent leaders from the outstanding companies we interviewed had a lot to say about the importance of tying metrics to methods to ensure accountability—and provide opportunities to celebrate success.

At Sodexo, for instance, former vice president of Global Diversity and Inclusion, Harris asks: "What, specifically are you looking at that informs that you're being successful? What are the business indicators that you're going to focus on, as well as the representation elements—identify the key things that matter in your organization." Then, she says, it's a matter of determining how you will hold people accountable. "Getting really specific about what that looks like will help you be more successful in getting there," she says.

Walmart's CDI scorecard measures all business areas and is a rollup of aggregated data points, says Fan. There are two big components in the scorecard: diversity metrics and culture and inclusion metrics. Diversity metrics focus on representation, promotion, and voluntary terminations. "Those are three very explicit metrics we measure for women and people of color," he says. On the inclusion and culture side, four specific metrics are used to measure: mentoring, education, culture index, and inclusion index. "It's a pulse survey to determine our associates' perceptions on sense of belonging, sense of fairness and sense of uniqueness." The scorecard is updated and reported on a quarterly basis, he says.

Along with measurement comes recognition, Harris stresses—internally and externally. At Sodexo, she says, strong relationships with external partners are critical for sourcing talent, for instance. She points to an active relationship with the National Organization on Disability as one of many examples. Best-in-class awards and other types of external recognition should also be leveraged and celebrated, she says.

For GM, says Barrett, both static and dynamic metrics are used to gauge the success and impact of inclusion efforts. "On the static side, I can look at what our participation rates are with our Employee Resource Groups," he says. Certainly, he's been able to demonstrate success with 36,000 employees engaged in these groups, up from 6,000 when he assumed his role.

Engagement scores, says Barrett, also provide a static means of gauging success. "I'm able to look at this by race, ethnicity, and gender, even LGBTQ. I'm also able to look at people with disabilities or veterans in the organization. You name it, and I'm able to see what the engagement rate is and to see if there are any hot spots, if you will—areas where I think we're lacking in engagement."

As we discussed earlier, based on their assessment of talent acquisition and the desire to draw top talent from an increasingly diverse North American talent pool, BASF recognized an opportunity for improvement. "We decided that we wanted to make sure that we were reflecting the full spectrum of the North American talent market in the decisions that we were making, so we put in place an aspirational goal that we were going to make sure that 50 percent of the people we interview for all of our roles reflect some element of diversity," Rossman says. Coupled with this, she says, "The company also put in place a requirement that the people doing the interviews reflected that level of diversity."

Aligned with Strategy

Inclusion metrics don't exist separately from other corporate metrics. Remember, inclusion is a business imperative. Consequently, it's important that these metrics are clearly tied to driving overall organizational performance.

At GM, says Barrett, the strategic focus for inclusion and diversity starts with the value proposition: "We want to be talent competitive for the best talent around the globe, and we want to be able to win in the marketplace—it's talent and market." This focus recognizes the critical link between staff demographics and market results, what we refer to as *Key Employee Demographics Required for Growth*. It's not just doing diversity as some kind of organizational exercise or initiative designed to be morally or ethically good. It's about business.

One of the key concepts that we emphasize in our work is the importance of focusing on these *Key Employee Demographics Required for Growth*. That means that as businesses work to focus on engaging new, younger audiences in their markets they *absolutely* need the input and insights from their employees who are part of these audiences.

Sodexo is one company that gets this. Their board is comprised of 50 percent women—women who, in most industries, represent at least 50 percent of the market. Attracting and developing talent that is tied to areas of market focus or expansion provides an alignment that keeps the business focus front and center. From a talent perspective, Barrett breaks his approach into four quadrants:

- The arenas where you're going to be active (e.g., the markets)
- The vehicles—how are you going to get there?
- Differentiators—what competitive advantages do you have?
- Staging—the sequence of your moves: what's the plan?

Continually, says Barrett, GM is in "assessment mode." The process, he says, involves "taking decisive action, and then from there it's into sustainment and accountability." But you don't just "keep it there forever," he says. "You take more action and more sustainment, always looking at accountability measures." After all, he notes, "As a manufacturing organization, we treasure what we measure!"

The process may sound straightforward and relatively simple, but it's anything but. The ability to be working a plan while simultaneously thinking about what else needs to be done is the mark of a strategic and nimble organization. It's a very vibrant and responsive approach. But, it's not an approach that Barrett, or GM's Employee Resource Groups, can own. It's an approach that must be owned and monitored from the top of the organization on down.

Mortenson also recognized the importance of tying accountability to inclusion efforts. "You have to hold people accountable for things you want to get done," says Weiss. "At the end of the day, accountability means that you did what you said you would do. It's not a 'gotcha'—it's about making sure that things are happening."

Tied to the Top

At GM, CEO Mary Barra's direct reports each have a diversity scorecard, focused on talent, which measures new hires, the diversity of new hires, and the diversity of the executive potential pool. It's about making sure that a sustainable pipeline is in place to fill potentially emerging roles and that this pipeline represents the desired diversity of the workforce and market.

Data is reviewed monthly, or quarterly, with a focus not on "trying to slam you for doing something wrong, but to be able to give you a picture of what's happening," says Barrett. "You're more apt to have success if you can actually see the data in front of you instead of just complaining after the fact." Data is power —the power to improve.

Organizations will not achieve an inclusive culture, and the results such a culture drives, without strong support and modeling of desired behaviors from the top of the organization. "On the culture side, we measure the perception of associates: does your leadership team demonstrate the core value of our culture?" says Fan of Walmart. Quarterly metrics allow the organization to see where changes are happening across the organization as well as in specific business units.

But, while measuring is important, it's not enough. Fan takes accountability one step further by "carrying on a conversation with the leaders to help them see what the data tells us—what are the hidden or missing links, and how are we going to course correct with a customized action plan for each business unit to make sure they address their challenges in a real-time manner." HR is involved in these discussions, which take place quarterly. "We work together to make sure we have the right plan in place and that we have implementation plans that explicitly and clearly map out targeted actions."

At Walmart, CEO Doug McMillon has been not only intentional but also highly visible and vocal about the company's quest for inclusion and has set a bold goal for the organization to achieve gender parity and racial parity by 2030. Walmart participates in the national initiatives for building more diverse organizations— Catalyst for Change[70]: CEO Action for Diversity & Inclusion and Paradigm for Parity[71].

At Michelin, Herb Johnson says, "At the end of the day, everyone within the company at every level, in every discipline, is responsible and accountable for diversity and inclusion." While he may be the Chief Diversity and Inclusion Officer (CDIO) for Michelin North America, Johnson is quick to point out that "I don't hire anyone, I don't fire anyone, and I don't promote anyone. Yet I have objectives around all of those things." That means, he says, that he must partner with the people who do all those things—with the hiring managers and with the leadership team—to make sure they are being accountable and that they understand why they're being accountable and what the benefit is of building a diverse workforce and making sure that the workforce is inclusive."

Not Just Internally Focused

A sound inclusion and diversity strategy isn't just focused on the internal environment, or an organization's employees. Forward-thinking companies also recognize that their supplier diversity strategies also impact their ability to attract and retain customers —and employees.

---

[70] https://bit.ly/2yxMFqb

[71] https://bit.ly/2IjJ0Hu

While much of our focus has been on employee inclusion and diversity, supplier diversity matters as well. At GM, for instance, Barrett says: "This is our 50th anniversary for supplier diversity. We're one of the first companies to actually have supplier diversity as a function, and we're very proud of how we work with minority suppliers and women suppliers."

GM also has a minority dealer development program that, says Barrett, is "the very first automotive to have that as an actual focus, and we're still the only automotive to have a women's dealer development program." GM has specific targets established to track their performance in these areas.

Mortenson Construction also has been a world-class leader in supplier diversity for a number of years.

Beyond suppliers, market considerations also come into play, says Sodexo's Harris. "D&I needs to be integrated into all functions and core business strategies not only in terms of how we think about our HR policies but how we go to market, as well as the products and services we offer," she says. This involves, she says, thinking about multicultural marketing in a diverse consumer space.

Bold Goals

To move the needle on inclusion and diversity, you need to know your current state. That means examining your current demographic makeup and identifying areas of opportunity for improvement. For Mortenson Construction, says Weiss, "what we found in the data is that on our operations side, we really needed to improve our representation in women and people of color." The situation was different, she says, on the business services side of the organization where there were plenty of women but an identified need for more people of color. Then goals needed to be established to drive change.

Michelin, says Johnson, is "pressing forward with new leadership." He's excited about the direction the company is headed and the ambitious goals they've established. In 2017, the company had a target of 45 percent diverse hires (women and people of color); in 2018, they've raised the bar to 50 percent. "It's a little bit of a stretch, but we're confident we'll get there," he says. "By 2022, we need to be around 60 percent diverse hires to make sure that we're able to fill the pipelines and have as diverse an organization as we possibly can."

Sodexo has also established bold goals. "Our goal is to have 40 percent of women represented in our senior leadership population by 2025, and we are also seeking to achieve 100 percent of our employees working within enterprises that have gender-balanced management."

Importantly, though, says Harris, while quantitative business metrics are crucial to support D&I work and illustrate tangible achievements, "the qualitative side is as, or sometimes more, important."

The strategy for creating a culture of inclusion starts at the top, says Harris. At Sodexo, that means global goals have been established and are being monitored by the global executive committee in partnership with the Global Chief Diversity Officer and the Chief People Officer.

But, the strategic focus on inclusion and diversity shouldn't stop at the top of the organization. While senior leadership needs to drive the vision and the strategy, and the Chief Human Resources Officer (CHRO) and CDIO need to ensure deployment, creating a culture of inclusion and belonging needs to be owned by the entire organization.

Smart companies are working to move leaders to a place where they can clearly see what strategic diversity looks like. It's not about compliance or "it's the right thing to do," but making these efforts part of a clearly articulated business case. They focus on identifying their challenges and then working collaboratively to close the gaps.

Michelin has refined its D&I strategy over time. Today, says Johnson, it includes six levers to help the company be more intentional about its D&I focus:

- A steering committee
- Diversity Councils and Business Resource Groups
- Recruitment
- Career management
- Employer branding
- Learning and development

Sodexo has constructed a governance model that has allowed it to have a variety of communication efforts driving the messages, starting with its Global Executive Committee and cascading down through the organization. Senior leaders who sit on the Global Executive Committee also serve on Sodexo's five global dimensions task forces, which include a focus on gender, LGBTQ, disability, cultures and origins, and generations. They serve as executive sponsors and, says Harris, "are very, very involved and engaged." That engagement, she says, "helps to expand not only their knowledge but the influence they have on how we get to drive the work into the global regions around the world."

Harris' D&I teams report to the Chief Diversity Officer (CDO) and are organized to support each of the company's global regions, partnering with regional D&I leaders who reside in the regions around the globe. These partnerships serve not only to build strong relationships but also to ensure alignment and consistent communication, allowing for local variations that recognize global cultural differences. "I know it might sound a bit complicated and complex," Harris says, "but it is working; it has served us very well in having feet on the ground in the middle, at the top, at all layers of the organization—to help drive awareness and accountability at the local level."

At Michelin, Johnson's team also is focused on strategy supported by strong and ongoing communication. Alignment with business objectives is also critical to ensure a business focus —again, inclusion is a business imperative first and foremost. Michelin's six levers are aligned with the business and supported by an effective communication plan. The strategy is a work in progress, Johnson says, but notes that "we have made incredible progress." The focus, he says, is on "creating and fostering a culture of inclusion through our shared purpose and business goal of 'ONE Michelin focused on the customer.'" The company is also working on putting dashboards in place to further drive accountability. "We want to be able to visibly assess our progress on D&I and really foster the partnerships and value and the importance this has with our customers."

Communication is an important part of an effective D&I strategy, especially for very large organizations. Sodexo is a prime example. Ensuring that the D&I message gets out to all employees in all locations regularly and accurately is no small feat, Harris acknowledges. "That's one of our key challenges," she says.

Building a strong business case for inclusion, says Harris, involves "clearly articulating strategies directly connected to the business. If you want to engage leaders in the work, and you haven't begun the journey, it's really important to speak their language and help them see the possibilities that diversity and inclusion can afford them in advancing their business objectives."

Tied to Rewards

Bold goals are great and a definite driver of result, but only if tied to some form of tangible recognition or rewards. It's an area of potential sensitivity, says Mortenson's Weiss.

"A lot of companies have sort of danced around 'do you tie financial rewards to improve D&I through a bonus program?' It's really sensitive and hard to think about. Nobody wants to believe that they're hired, and somebody makes a bonus—that's not the message we wanted to send at all." Instead, she says, Mortenson has experimented with the idea of rewarding leaders for achieving D&I goals. "We've taken the focus off hard numbers because we don't like some of the unintended consequences that can happen. Instead, we say, 'Tell us about what you've done and how you've moved your business forward.'" Then an assessment is done based on a grid Mortenson has developed. "We decide, from there, how they will be evaluated," says Weiss.

Sodexo, as we've seen, has also tied rewards to results for diversity and inclusion metrics. Still, says Harris, qualitative metrics shouldn't be overlooked. In fact, she says, "Rohini [Rohini Anand, Sodexo's SVP of Corporate Responsibility and Global Chief Diversity Officer] has even said that if she had it to do over again, she would have led with the qualitative early and then added the quantitative, because you have to take managers on a journey to help them understand the "why" behind the movement."

11 The Need to Build Inclusive Leader Competencies with Unconscious Bias and Inclusion Behaviors

In one executive session after another, we have the opportunity to interact with some extremely humble and very bright leaders. We often review with them career disparity data that we've gathered, as previously discussed. As we do, what we always find so striking is how dumbfounded these exceptional leaders are about *why* there are such disparities within their organizations. These highly intelligent and accomplished leaders can *not* get their arms around why there is a fall-off for women immediately, for instance. In fact, they are often quite puzzled by this. Was it because women had children? Was it because women started in administrative positions? How could this possibly be?

I'm quite sure if the environment was safe enough, plenty of women or people of color could explain it to them.

None of them considered that there is systemic bias that occurs in most companies at every step. Bias is an extremely difficult concept to grapple with because no one would intend to make life more difficult for any group. I have found that generally people are well intentioned.

And yet, year after year and decade after decade, we keep replicating the same pattern. Let's start with understanding what bias is.

Unconscious Bias: A Leader's Greatest Liability

It is part of the human condition to have biases and to allow those biases to shape our behavior every day. A bias represents a cognitive shortcut. It is the autopilot in our cognitive operating system. If we didn't have biases, it would be difficult to function because some of the biases we have simply reflect learned assumptions made over time that are useful for everyday life: red means danger and green means go. In fact, there are four major categories of cognitive bias—social, memory, decision-making, and probability or belief bias—that together make up 104 different cognitive biases.

Many social biases limit our effectiveness as leaders, and it is specifically our *unconscious* biases about those who are different from us that undermine our leadership potential.

One of the social biases most relevant for leaders is called in-group bias—the tendency for people to give preferential treatment to others they perceive to be members of their own group. Another important bias is called the self-fulfilling prophecy—a positive or negative expectation about situations or people that affects a person's behavior, causing those expectations to be fulfilled.

The best example of in-group bias is a tendency to elevate the skills or capabilities of someone who holds a college degree from our alma mater or a prestigious Ivy League school. Another is to default to the solution that your department has proposed over that of another department's view. These are examples of in-group bias.

One of the most well documented examples of the self-fulfilling prophecy comes from an experiment a school teacher named Jane Elliot did in the mid-1960s. She divided her class into children with brown eyes and blue eyes and told them on different days that one group was smarter, better, and nicer than the other. In a documentary called "Eye of the Storm" that was created by William Peters in 1970 for ABC News, viewers saw that Elliot simply behaving differently toward these children reduced their participation in class, reduced their performance on simple tests, and increased their irritability. It has become one of the most discussed experiments in the power of performance expectations and how it applies in educational and workplace settings.

What makes in-group bias and the self-fulfilling prophecy effect so problematic for leaders is that these are part of a growing list of unconscious biases—implicit assumptions we make about others based on past experiences. Emerging research about unconscious biases suggests that they are pervasive and that they do influence behavior. Furthermore, implicit or unconscious biases can negatively impact decisions about employees' potential for success, even in the face of evidence to suggest the person meets or exceeds expectations.

In the U.S., most individuals have grown up seeing and experiencing a legacy of historical references toward African-

Americans, Latinos, Asians, women, and members of the LGBTQ community—negative and positive. Our collective experiences and exposure to major events in the continued dialogue on social and economic justice—slavery, civil rights, religious freedom, same sex marriage, and other hot button issues—frame and influence our thinking about these groups. Unconscious bias can, thus, influence who to select for key teams, who to nominate for advancement, and who to trust in front of a client—even if we think of ourselves as fair or egalitarian.[72]

Our Bias about Unconscious Bias

At InclusionINC, we have a bias about unconscious bias. We think the only way to do bias work is to pair it with inclusive leader competencies. In essence, let's all acknowledge we have biases, identify the areas we need to work on, and find a way to change our behaviors and build our skills. Then we can have open discussions about how unconscious bias impacts our decision-making process, particularly in talent development.

To that end, we have done extensive work to validate our inclusion behaviors and inclusive leader competencies. The data we gathered in our customized InclusionINC inclusion and diversity assessment work of 310,000 employees throughout Corporate America has helped me define the business behaviors that reflect inclusion. And, guess what? It's not rocket science. These are simple behaviors. For example, when we asked participants when they feel most included, the number one response was "When I'm asked my opinion".

This doesn't have to be a big deal. Business behaviors that support inclusion don't have to involve ambitious rewards and recognition programs. These behaviors can be as simple as two powerful words: "Thank you."

Behaviors that support inclusion involve taking the time to listen —not just telling people what to do. When changes occur, behaviors that support inclusion involve giving people the rationale for why certain decisions have been made and, better

---

[72] Inclusive Leader 360: Reducing the Impact of Unconscious Bias. An InclusionINC Whitepaper. Engelmeier, Hernandez, Johnson.

yet, inviting their input as part of the decision-making process. Behaviors that support inclusion allow decision-making down to the associate or very junior level. These behaviors encourage involvement at every tier within the organization and from every individual in the organization.

We did the same with inclusive leader skills.

Inclusive Leader Skills

What do inclusive leader behaviors look like? Based on our research, we've identified 12 inclusive leadership competencies that were covered in my 2014 book, "Becoming an Inclusive Leader—How to Navigate the 21st Century Global Workforce."[73] Here's the list. How many of these traits do you possess? How may do your leaders, managers and supervisors possess?

1. Ego management. To what extent are you able to control your urge to be the smartest person in the room?
2. Open to a wide range of inputs. Do you gather input from a wide range of diverse sources before forming an opinion or making a decision?
3. Intellectual curiosity. Are you continually attuned to, and positively impacted by, the conditions, events, and circumstances around you?
4. Transparency. Are you open, direct, and honest with others?
5. Emotional intelligence. How well do you perceive emotions, reason with emotions, understand emotions, and manage emotions?
6. Futurecasting. How adept are you at accurately predicting the future and its potential impact on your business?
7. Humility. Are you able to admit that you're wrong?
8. Cultural agility. How well do you interact with people from other cultures, within and outside of the U.S.?
9. Collaboration. Are you able to work inclusively with others, working together toward a desired endpoint?
10. Accessibility. Do you make yourself available to others, and are you willing to listen to their feedback?
11. Diversity of thought. How well do you avoid groupthink?

---

[73] https://amzn.to/2zYMHsM

12. Adaptability. Do you have the ability to assess the conditions and circumstances around you and adapt to change on an ongoing basis?

How do we build these skills among our leaders—and seek them in those we hire or promote to leadership positions? It's an intentional process, says Mortenson's Weiss. At Mortenson, she says, "it was a very strategic decision to try to translate the buy-in that we saw at our executive or senior leadership team to what we call our business group leaders who lead all of our business lines. They're the frontline to each of those business units. If those group leaders weren't able to truly show inclusive behaviors, we knew we would not be able to make progress."

To make this happen and really bake inclusive leadership skills into the fiber of their group leaders, Weiss says, "We got a little tricky." In 2017, Mortenson said their group leaders would be responsible for bringing content about inclusion and diversity to their groups. That, she says, "encouraged them to learn more about it and to lead those conversations." Making group leaders accountable, she says, was more impactful than simply having them sit in a classroom. "They had to digest it and make sure it became part of what they understood and believed—they had to walk the talk."

BASF took the important step in opening conversations with both leaders and employees about what inclusion looks and feels like from a leadership perspective through a business case challenge. "They had 36 hours to come up with some solutions and then presented them to a highly diverse and divergent group of leaders. What I love about it is that some are ideas I would not have come up with—they're truly coming from a different perspective, and I love that!"

The Impact of Unconscious Bias and Using Inclusive Leader Competencies to be more Effective

Let's forget about neurology for a minute and return to some baseline awareness of unconscious bias. Let's couple this with a look at which inclusive leader competencies a leader can work on to make changes.

A SHRM survey of recruiters conducted in 2017, and covered for SHRM by Roy Maurer[74], revealed that male recruiters are more likely to judge candidates on appearance. Here's what the survey results revealed.

Appearance Matters—In Ways We May Not Even Realize!

One of the most interesting findings was the difference in how male and female recruiters take a candidate's appearance into account during the interview process. "Male recruiters said they tend to pay more attention to appearance, personal style, and enthusiasm during the screening process," reports Maurer. According to the research, males are more likely than females to look at applicants' photos prior to the interview. Males also admit they're likely to be influenced by the photos they view. They're also more likely than female interviewers to reject a candidate that they feel is "wearing attire considered too casual" to an interview, Maurer writes. Female recruiters, says Maurer, focused more on candidates' educational background and references than on appearance.

The Pervasive Impacts of Unconscious Bias

SHRM's survey results support the presence, and pervasiveness, of unconscious bias. "Half of surveyed recruiters (57 percent) believe unconscious bias is part of the typical hiring process, and some respondents say they've witnessed biased attitudes in action," reports Maurer. "About a fourth (27 percent) of recruiters say they have observed or heard sexist attitudes expressed toward a candidate, and 22 percent said the same about racist attitudes."

The fact that so many respondents said they believe bias is present in the recruiting process is likely due to the fact that they believe they are observing such behavior in others, as opposed to themselves. It's important for all of us to recognize that we, too, suffer from unconscious bias and to be alert to that potential in all our interactions.

The SHRM survey is another wake-up call reflecting the fact that unconscious bias has real-world impacts that can't be ignored.

---

[74] https://bit.ly/2iebS4B

Recruiters are gatekeepers in so many ways; their attitudes and biases have big implications for the level of inclusion and diversity in organizations of all kinds.

Building Inclusive Leadership Competencies

In "Becoming an Inclusive Leader," we outlined some specific actions that organizations, and their leaders, can take to build inclusive leadership skills among their leaders, managers, supervisors, and, frankly, *all* staff members.

Strong communication skills are clearly foundational for becoming inclusive leaders. We're not alone in our thinking here. A study conducted by the Economist Intelligence Unit and sponsored by Lucidchart, titled "Communication Barriers in the Modern Workplace,"[75] found that "across the board, employees believe miscommunication is contributing to their stress, failure to complete projects and loss of sales," according to an article in Chief Learning Officer[76].

The companies that are really leveraging the diversity of their organizations through inclusion recognize that inclusion starts at the top. Inclusive leadership competencies are must haves to ensure an inclusive culture. But a case must be made to senior leadership, so they understand that inclusion is a business imperative and only inclusive leaders can help drive the business forward.

At Mortenson, says Weiss, "We were able to bring the case for inclusion and diversity to our leadership team. It made such sense to them because we tied it to our people. That was one of my big takeaways. In every company there are things that really matter to that company. At Mortenson, the thing that really matters to us is our people. We said, 'If we're going to get a great ROI, our leaders would appreciate that, but what they appreciate even more is that this matters to our people and helping our people be more successful.'"

Training certainly has a critical role to play here, and those companies that have committed to improving their inclusive

---

[75] https://bit.ly/2OTJ2Vn

[76] https://bit.ly/2RAjZFx

leadership competencies have been those to reap reward. Michelin is a prime example. Discussions related to unconscious bias have been particularly impactful, says Michelin's Johnson. "It's the cornerstone of what we're doing here. I probably get more feedback on that portion of the training and the importance of it. It's probably been the biggest 'aha moment' that I think we've gotten from the training that really helps build our culture of inclusion." Raising awareness hasn't been a "giant leap for people because of our strong culture but making them aware and making the tie to diversity and inclusion has helped us make a lot of progress in a short period of time."

12 THE CHALLENGE TO LEADERS

What if you as a leader were given an approach that had a high likelihood of improving profitability by 21–33 percent? Would you consider it? What if McKinsey, a trusted advisor and counselor to many of the world's most influential businesses and institutions, presented you with a business case to improve value creation by 27 percent? What would you do? See the two charts below that make the point very plainly.

As the smart leaders that you are, I think you'd do it. The answer in the case of these two questions would be to get women on the executive team. This may be a Herculean task based on how you look today. Yet, I believe you should go after it. As this data from McKinsey illustrates, the investment is well worth it![77]

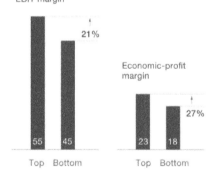

Gender diversity on executive teams is strongly correlated with profitability and value creation.

Likelihood of financial performance above national industry median, %

Gender diversity of executive team by quartile[1]

EBIT margin[2]

21%

Economic-profit margin

27%

55   45   23   18

Top Bottom   Top Bottom

[1]Results are statistically significant at p-value <0.05.
[2]Average earnings-before-interest-and-taxes (EBIT) margin.

McKinsey&Company

---

[77] https://mck.co/2DPv3YP

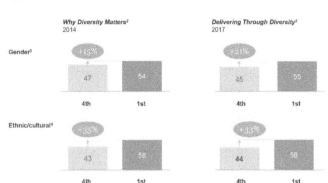

Likelihood of financial performance[1] above national industry median by diversity quartile
Percent

Why Diversity Matters[2]
2014

Delivering Through Diversity[2]
2017

Gender[3]

+15% 47 (4th) 54 (1st)

+21% 45 (4th) 55 (1st)

Ethnic/cultural[4]

+35% 43 (4th) 58 (1st)

+33% 44 (4th) 59 (1st)

1 Average EBIT margin, 2010–13 in *Why Diversity Matters* and 2011–15 in *Delivering Through Diversity*
2 2014 results are statistically significant at p-value <0.1; 2017 results are statistically significant at p-value <0.05
3 Gender executive data, for 2014, N = 383; for 2017, N = 991
4 Ethnic/cultural executive data, for 2014, N = 364; for 2017, N = 589

NOTE: Percentages shown here are rounded to the nearest whole number; however, calculation of the differentials in quartile performance uses actual decimal values

SOURCE: McKinsey Diversity Matters database

Now what if you had an even stronger financial case? What if you as a leader were given an approach that had a high likelihood of improving profitability by 33 percent? Would you consider it? What if you were presented with a business case to improve value creation by 43 percent? Again, you would take action, right?

Here's the greatest business opportunity you've been given in decades. It's not only an opportunity; it's actually a mandate based on what's happening with unemployment right now.

Here is how some of our esteemed thought leaders spoke about the leader's challenge.

It's a process not a destination, as Michelin has learned, says Johnson. The company has already gone through an extensive series of training sessions around inclusive leadership and inclusion as a business strategy, says Johnson. "That's been foundational for us," he says. In fact, he says, effectively participating in the training is "one of the indicators that we use to identify talent."

Importantly, though, Johnson notes, leaders must be willing to let go of their top talent—to let them learn, grow and sometimes go. "What we find is that, because they appreciate the diverse perspectives of their departments or their teams, they don't want to lose it," he says. That can lead to some people becoming stuck, but he's mindful of the potential and says, "I have to focus on making sure people aren't being stuck because they're perceived as too valuable to let go when, in fact, we have to allow them to continue to progress and grow."

To avoid the stuck state that we talked about previously, organizational leaders need to be constantly vigilant.

At Mortenson, says Weiss, the stuck state has not yet been an issue, although she acknowledges it may be at some point. "I think where other organizations can get stuck is in not continuing the conversation on inclusion and diversity or in considering these efforts as a program. We've learned that it takes continual conversation—it needs to be part of the fabric of not only the culture but also the systems underneath the culture."

Avoiding the stuck state requires continual vigilance, agrees GM's Barrett. "At GM, I think we do a lot of great things, but we always have more work to do. I think it's important not to be locked in time, not to rest on your laurels, but to continue to look at ways to be able to innovate, not only in our products and what we do in the marketplace but in how we manage our talent."

Weiss makes an important point for other companies that may be experiencing their own stuck state: inclusion is everyone's responsibility. "We decided early on that we didn't want to carve out one person to be responsible for D&I because we were worried that it would then give everybody else a pass. Our Chief Operating Officer (COO) is truly our leader of this work—I just get the opportunity to help." By embedding responsibility for inclusion into the overall culture of the organization, says Weiss, it becomes everybody's job—because it is!

Sodexo has a particularly compelling story to tell because they came from an entirely different place to begin their journey of inclusion—a place of mass media attention on a lawsuit that resulted in an $80 million payout.[78]

Unlike other places where she has worked, said Harris, "I was shocked that here at Sodexo, they named it out loud—they took

---

[78] https://fxn.ws/2yo2AXM

it very seriously to heart that this was never going to happen again and really committed to making changes."

"We've often been asked to tell our story," says Harris. It's a story that has a very happy ending. "We have a very strong D&I culture that allows us to be benchmarked often," says Harris. It's a story that has been made possible by a concerted focus and commitment from senior leaders. "Top down commitment is really critical—absolutely critical," says Harris. "That really helps an organization keep it out in front by defining the business imperative associated with why D&I matters and what will be done to monitor, reward, and hold people accountable."

Complacency, says Harris, can lead to plateaus. "We're always looking for the next big thing."

For organizations that may be just starting their journey toward an inclusive culture, or those needing a reset, Walmart's Fan recommends starting with an assessment of "current state"—that lays the foundation for where you will go and the establishment of key metrics that will help you track progress and celebrate milestones.

"Whenever you have that objective state in mind, then you can determine your strategic focus areas." Organizations have limited resources, Fan acknowledges. "You need to make tradeoff decisions to see what low-hanging fruit may be out there that you can tackle immediately in the short-term, and then, after you've selected the focal points, the next step will be designing the programs and process to get you where you want to go." Part of that, he says, should be an execution plan—"the roadmap and playbook and how you're going to leverage each of the stakeholders internally to make it happen, and make it sustainable."

The process doesn't just sit at leadership levels, though, Fan stresses. "You've got to figure out a way, through different programmatic efforts, to engage and enlist everyone on this journey."

Diversity is important, but it's just a starting point. It's not enough in and of itself. We have gone through too many years, focusing on the numbers, proudly pointing to the inroads we've made in terms of recruiting women and people of color. And yet, when it comes right down to it, we haven't been successful *engaging* women and people of color through *inclusion*. Inclusion is the business imperative—not diversity!

That's something that Rossman keeps a firm focus on in her work at BASF. "We're not looking to hire someone because they're diverse. We're looking to hire the best talent, recognizing that often the best talent is talent that's diverse, given the great diversity of the North American talent market. We're truly looking to attract the best men and women—the best people of all backgrounds—to BASF."

Inclusion is a business strategy. It's a strategy that must focus on connecting internal and external audiences to sell more goods and services. Doing this well—getting beyond the stuck state— will help to drive results with clients and customers. In fact, in the environment we now find ourselves in, a rich environment comprised of many different faces and many different viewpoints, it's the only way. Start crafting a strategy for inclusion and committing to creating a culture of accountability. Then work with your board, senior executives, senior leaders and staff up and down every silo in your organization to break down the silos, open minds, remove barriers and begin the hard work of embracing inclusion to drive change.

BIOS

Ken Barrett is Chief Diversity Officer at GM, a post he's held since 2012. Barrett has more than two decades of executive experience, including five years of award-winning performance as the U.S. Navy's Diversity Director. He also has served as the Undersecretary of Defense's Acting Director, Office of Diversity Management and Equal Opportunity, and spent 28 years in the U.S. Navy.

Donald Fan is Senior Director in the Global Office of Culture, Diversity, and Inclusion, with Walmart. He grew up in Shanghai, China, and came to the United States for graduate studies, later joining Walmart in what was then called the Technology Information division. He transferred over to the Office of Diversity, which was established in 2003, and has stayed in that space since. Fan says: "During my tenure in this role, I've been responsible for leading the efforts in many different areas such as strategy, analytics, program development, business insights/ intelligence, external relations, and communications and marketing."

Sandy Harris is the former Vice President of Global Diversity and Inclusion at Sodexo. Harris' career has spanned more than 25 years—she has worked in six Fortune 500 companies and has a variety of background and experiences that she pulls from.

Herb Johnson, Jr., is Chief Diversity and Inclusion Officer for Michelin North America, a role he's held since January 2014. He joined BFGoodrich Tires in 1977, holding a number of positions in research and development. In 1988, he transferred to the marketing department in the high-performance tire and motorsport division. In 1990, Michelin purchased BFGoodrich, and in 1995 he relocated to Greenville, South Carolina, Michelin's North American headquarters. From 1996 to 2002, he was the North American Director of Motorsport for the Michelin and BFGoodrich brands. In 2002, he took an assignment in sales and was responsible for the independent dealer network. Prior to his current assignment, he worked as Director of Community Relations for seven years.

Patricia Rossman is the Chief Diversity and Inclusion Officer at BASF, where she has responsibility for strategy creation and driving BASF in North America to achieve one of its fundamental goals—to be a company truly known for the diversity and inclusion of its workforce.

Molly Weiss is Senior Director of Human Resources with Mortenson Construction in Minneapolis, a construction and development company with about 5,000 team members nationwide. Weiss has been with the company for nearly 7 years; prior to that, she worked at both Fortune 500 and smaller companies in, primarily, HR generalist roles—focused on helping companies determine how to get the best from their people and how to help people do their very best in their work.

About the Author

Shirley Engelmeier's groundbreaking work in the area of Inclusion and Diversity has been a catalyst for change, spurring others to embrace her philosophy that inclusion is a business imperative. Engelmeier is a consultant to the C-Suite, linking inclusion work to companies' strategic priorities. This is not a "nice to do," but a "must do" for businesses in the 21st century hoping to gain and maintain a competitive edge.

Engelmeier has been working to meet client outcomes as an inclusion and diversity strategist and consultant for more than 25 years. Prior to that, she held senior management positions in global consumer product organizations Brown & Williamson and Frito-Lay. She has pioneered inclusion and diversity initiatives that have had a major impact on improving business results through more engaged employees, breakthrough innovation and the retention of top talent. She and the pioneering InclusionINC team she leads have moved the field of inclusion and diversity from tactics to strategy through their proprietary InclusionSCORECARD®.

In her work to confirm the business case for inclusion, Engelmeier has led the charge to globally validate inclusion behaviors and inclusive leader competencies. Moving beyond pop-culture hype, she leads the field in groundbreaking work to help senior executives excel by integrating the exploration of unconscious bias with the development of inclusive leader competencies through an Inclusive Leader 360 and executive learning sessions.

A highly regarded business strategist, Engelmeier has consulted with Fortune 1000 companies and emerging enterprises on inclusion and diversity initiatives across many industries, working with companies including Michelin, BASF, ESPN, Denny's, Intuitive Surgical, SCI, 3M, and Mortenson Construction, to name a few. Originally trained as an educator, Engelmeier earned her B.S. degree from the University of Minnesota and resides with her family in Minneapolis.

CPSIA information can be obtained
at www.ICGtesting.com
Printed in the USA
BVHW082055291119

565159BV00002B/37/P